POTATOES

Other books in
The Particular Palate™ Cookbook series

GARLIC
by Sue Kreitzman

RIBS
by Susan Friedland

TAILGATE PARTIES
by Susan Wyler

COOKIES
by Diane Rozas and Rosalee Harris

DELI
by Sue Kreitzman

CHICKEN BREASTS
by Diane Rozas

CHOCOLATE CANDY
by Anita Prichard

COMFORT FOOD
by Sue Kreitzman

FISH STEAKS AND FILLETS
by Michele Scicolone

SAUCES AND DRESSINGS
by Diane Rozas

POTATOES

68 Delicious Recipes for Everyone's Favorite Vegetable

by Sue Kreitzman

A Particular Palate Cookbook™
Harmony Books/New York

For Sandy Williams
my best potato-loving friend

A Particular Palate Cookbook

Copyright © 1989 by Sue Kreitzman

Published by Harmony Books, a division of Crown Publishers, Inc., 225 Park Avenue South, New York, New York 10003

HARMONY, PARTICULAR PALATE, and colophon are trademarks of Crown Publishers, Inc.

Manufactured in the United States of America

Library of Congress Cataloging-in-Publication Data
Kreitzman, Sue.
    Potatoes.

    "A Particular palate cookbook."
    Includes index.
    1. Cookery (Potatoes)   I. Title.
TX803.P8K68 1989   641.6′521   88–16524
ISBN 0-517-57118-8

10 9 8 7 6 5 4 3 2 1
First Edition

Contents

Acknowledgments

Thank you to Barbara Bradford, friendly typist, who moved away all too soon, and to my indispensable and beloved staff: Rosemarie Espley, secretary extraordinaire; Sandie Perry, talented and dazzlingly organized kitchen helper, and Mary Hardy, who always cheerfully lends a helping hand even in semiretirement.

And tons of heartfelt thanks to my husband, Steve, and son, Shawm, who—as always—support, encourage, and love me to pieces.

Introduction

"The early history of the potato was set on a stage dominated by the mysterious grandeur of the Andes, whose dread influence could never have been long absent from the thought and actions of the men who, thousands of years before the coming of Columbus, won for all mankind this and other priceless gifts from the recesses of nature's storehouse."

RADCLIFFE SOLOMON
The History and Social Influence of the Potato,
1949

My most intense potato experience occurred when I was a rank newcomer to England, driving from Biggleswade to Bury St. Edmunds, on a miserable, foggy and drizzly day. Driving on the left-hand side of the road caused profound and anguished concentration. There was a miasma in the car, composed of that anguish, general grumpiness about a mammoth bread-baking session I had just completed in Biggleswade that had not gone particularly well, and the fog itself, which seemed to be *everywhere,* including inside the car. So, there I was—murky, disgruntled, speeding down what seemed like the wrong side of a road I could not see very well, wishing desperately that I were back in my home. Roundabouts, that bane of British roadways, were rather confusing to me at that time, so given the weather and the general state of my mind, I inevitably missed a turn off. Suddenly I was: Lost in the Fens.

The road was a narrow, rough track running interminably through a bleak and insubstantial landscape. Apparently, some dark and malevolent force was out to get me, because snarling young men in camouflage suits kept looming out of the fog, brandishing bayonets. A shadowy presence trundling along just ahead of my car lurched and rocked over the bumpy road and released, at irregular intervals, large missiles that flew at the car and scattered what was left of my wits. Surely I had stumbled into a sinister parallel universe, where home and sunshine and common sense did not exist, where benevolence was unknown, and where all the forces of nature were evil. But for a moment the fog swirled away and the mysterious missile-throwing vehicle became substantial enough to identify. It was a rickety old lorry, overflowing with potatoes—huge, misshapen, earth-encrusted fen potatoes. Every once in a while the lorry hit a rut and a potato was hurled off the teetering pile.

Potatoes! A universe that contained potatoes could not be sinister. A universe containing potatoes has to be benevolent and sensible, right down to the (foggy) ground. I stopped the car and jumped out to gather a few of the earthy tubers. A camouflaged young man appeared and smiled. The army was on training maneuvers, he explained. Miserable day for it, too. As we chatted, rays of watery sunshine appeared. Suddenly, the fens looked almost cheerful. And on such a narrow road, there's not that much difference between the left and the right side anyway—so why worry?

I was back home in no time, and the potatoes were scrubbed and popped into a hot oven. Later feasting on the delicious steaming spuds (cut open and mashed roughly with Parmesan cheese, buttermilk, and freshly ground pepper), I mused that a universe that delivers free potatoes out of the fog is the perfect universe for me.

PRE-COLUMBIAN POTATOES Potatoes have been around for at least 8,000 years. They originated in the Andes of South America, and eventually became a significant staple—spiritual, economic, and nutritional—of the Inca Empire. The potatoes of the Incas were varied as to size and color, ranging from peanut size to about the size of a medium Idaho baker of today; from red and gold to blue, gray, even black. Today, in the highlands of Peru, a potato-lover will still find dozens of varieties of potatoes in assorted colors and sizes in the markets.

Until very recently, potato-lovers in the United States and in England could only dream wistfully of such tuberous variety; a spud-seeking visit to the supermarket might yield, depending on time of year and location, new potatoes, a single variety of waxy "old" potatoes, a red-skinned variety, and

FEAR OF FOOD

Someday, a gastronomically curious astronaut will return home from his travels with a cargo bay stuffed full of a lumpy, oddly colored Venusian swamp root. It will be the most delicious and sensuous food yet discovered, versatile as to cooking methods that can be applied to it, beautifully complemented by earthly herbs and spices, and deeply soothing to the human psyche. The nutrition of this unusual root will be so perfect that it will virtually burst with vital trace minerals and vitamins that no one has even *heard* of yet. And to complete its perfection, the root will grow inexpensively, quickly, and with a minimum of labor. Will the populace embrace this exemplary foodstuff and make it a staple that nourishes the Third World, comforts the affluent, and delights the culinary intelligentsia? Of course not. Oh, the quirkier gourmets—those few twisted masters and mistresses of the decadent palate, who revel in cuttlefish-ink meringues and two-year-old white truffles and long to taste *Amanita phalloides* on toast—they will laud the new root, with their beady eyes gleaming and their pasty cheeks quivering, but everyone else will shun it. The FDA will shriek in terror, the government will pass laws against it, religious leaders will preach hysterical sermons warning of the lust-engendering "root of all evil," and pregnant women will avoid all contact with it lest it cause them to give birth to monsters.

Not likely, you say? Consider the potato and its inauspicious debut into Europe. Not only was it considered an evil and decadent food—one that would cause frenzied lust followed by death—but pregnant women thought that an evening meal of potatoes would cause their babies to be born with abnormally tiny heads. Some French botanists were convinced that growing the tubers would destroy the soil, and various medical experts linked it to a whole catalogue of physical ailments, from leprosy to syphilis, scrofula to rickets, consumption to rampant flatulence. In America, an influx of Irish immigrants introduced the potato to Londonderry, New Hampshire, in 1719. But by the mid-eighteenth century, many New Englanders, despite the Irish example, believed spuds to be an unhealthy food that inevitably shortened the natural life span. Before you feel too smug about your modern potato savvy, consider the very recent belief that the potato—that nutritional marvel—was *fattening* and full of starchy, worthless calories. How ridiculous. And how wonderful to luxuriate in potato plenty now, in the face of modern dietetic knowledge. So, enjoy. Eat all the spuds you want without fear, but do watch out for those Venusian roots.

perhaps a floury baking variety. Often, the bakers and the boilers were not labeled, and it was anyone's guess which potato would mash well, which would stay firm in salads, and which would produce fluffy baked flesh. (And often, the "new" potatoes were actually a year old and the red-skinned ones were dyed.) But burgeoning food consciousness and a growing appreciation for old cultivars are changing the potato situation in both countries. In the United States, greenmarkets and supermarkets are beginning to offer fascinating potato varieties, odd in color (to our modern eyes) and deep and vibrant in flavor. Open almost any edition of *The New Yorker* or one of the foodie magazines, and enticing ads invite you to send away for blue, yellow, or golden potatoes, or other rediscovered older cultivars beautifully packaged in burlap or baskets.

In England, one chain of upmarket supermarkets already offers—in addition to familiar cultivars—the beautiful firm and waxy Pink Fir and another, the French La Ratte with its lovely, vaguely chestnut flavor. But most extraordinary is the vision of the Safeway chain in England: they offer—over the four seasons—at least forty varieties of waxy and floury potatoes, labeling them "as carefully as fine wines and cheeses," in addition to providing advice on cooking methods for each variety. Safeway is commissioning farmers to grow a wondrous array of spuds, including those with blue, black, and red flesh.

So dry your jealous tears and abandon your longing to plunder the Andean markets when you can get your hands on both the money and the courage to smuggle interesting potatoes back home, hidden in your socks. If the current trend continues, a simple trip to your local supermarket may yield a spud bonanza. A new potato era is dawning.

WHO INTRODUCED THE POTATO TO EUROPE?

It wasn't Sir Walter Raleigh, and it wasn't Sir Francis Drake, although much romantic folklore attributes the momentous introduction to one or the other. Most likely, it was a nameless but ethnobotanically curious Spanish sailor who, in the sixteenth century, brought samples of the Incas' staff of life home to Spain from the highlands of the Andes. As often happened with foodstuffs from the New World, potatoes were met with reactions of revulsion and distrust. People throughout Europe refused to have anything to do with the strange tubers; they were believed to be evil, decadent, and as poisonous as their relative, deadly nightshade. Over the years, three important influences helped to establish potatoes as a delicious, wholesome, and highly nutritious food: Frederick the Great sent the armed military into a small Prussian town to convince the starving peasants to eat potatoes; August Parmentier served elegant French all-potato feasts to the elite of several continents (Ben Franklin attended one of these legendary dinners) and presented Marie Antoinette with potato blossoms to wear in her hair; and the Irish—the first to accept the mysterious tuber—physically flourished on their potatoes, until the entire crop was decimated by the tragic blight of 1846.

POTATO TYPES Although potatoes come in hundreds of varieties, there are basically two categories: waxy and floury. Waxy potatoes are comparatively low in starch and stay firm when cooked; they are best for boiling and steaming. Use steamed waxy spuds for potato salads, pan sautés, and hash browns.

Floury potatoes are starchier and have a fluffy texture when cooked. The Idaho Russet is the superstar of American floury potatoes. The long Russet Burbank, grown in Idaho's volcanic soil, is a potato in a million. Although I now live in English potato-growing country and have developed a deep affection for the local fen potatoes, I still miss the Idaho Russet with all my heart. Use floury potatoes for baking, mashing, frying and oven frying, and gratins.

New potatoes are any variety of immature potato that goes straight to market after harvest and not into storage. New potatoes may be small (tiny ones are called culls; they are an exquisite treat) or medium size, and they may be waxy or floury. To test if a potato is *really* new, rub the skin with your thumb; it should easily flake away.

Potato Test: If you have a potato that confuses you—is it waxy or floury?—use this testing method from Harold Mcgee's *On Food and Cooking:* Make a brine of 2 parts water, 1 part salt. Drop the potato in. If it is waxy, it will float; a floury potato is denser and will sink.

CHOOSING AND STORING POTATOES

Buy potatoes that are unblemished. Avoid those that are cracked, bruised, flabby, or mottled

THE SWEET POTATO MYSTERY

There are many forms of yam (*Dioscorea alata*)—greater yam, yellow yam, white yam, winged yam, hard yam—and not one of them is a sweet potato. Despite this fact, sweet potatoes, in the United States, are often sold under the misnomer yam. To confuse you even more, let me hasten to say that a sweet potato is not a potato. Potatoes (*Solanum tuberosum*) belong to the nightshade family; sweet potatoes (*Ipomoea batatas*) is a member of the morning glory family. But although the sweet potato is not really a potato, it takes beautifully to baking, mashing, and oven frying. Baked or mashed sweet potatoes are exquisite when beaten with a bit of rum or fresh orange juice, a touch of honey, and a sprinkling of 1 or 2 of the sweet curry spices: allspice, cinnamon, cardamom, coriander, and so on. Just be sure to avoid those awful recipes that call for canned sweet potatoes, maple syrup, brown sugar, and melted miniature marshmallows. Just thinking about such abominations makes my teeth ache.

with green. Green spots are indications of solanine, which develops upon exposure to light. A greenish potato will be bitter and will make you ill if you eat it. Either discard greenish potatoes or cut out the green portions with a paring knife.

Store potatoes loosely covered and unwashed in a coolish (45-50°F.) dark, dry place. Colder temperatures make the potatoes sweet (the starches turn to sugars), so don't refrigerate them. Warmer temperatures make the potatoes sprout and wither.

GUILT-FREE SPUDS How often have I heard someone say, "No potatoes for me, please, they are too fattening." What a vile calumny on the noble spud. People who work at maintaining their weight should embrace potatoes, wallow in them, rejoice in their variety and versatility. A medium potato contains no fat, has about 90 calories, and offers a good measure of niacin; vitamins A, C, B_1, and B_6; iron; potassium; and fiber. Potatoes are satisfying and filling; a meal of the tubers leaves you feeling that you have dined well and copiously. If you have a weight problem and are foolish enough to sabotage this exemplary foodstuff with butter, cream, and high-fat cheeses, you deserve every excess pound you gain. Apply common sense to spud cookery: use buttermilk, yogurt, mustard, stock, and medium and low-fat cheeses in place of high-fat ingredients. You can dine on the tubers happily and guilt free for the rest of your life.

Many of the recipes in this book are extremely low in fat, although they taste *nothing* like (shudder) diet food. For those of you who, like me, have a tendency to plunge headlong into obesity when the butter and oil flow, these low-fat recipes have been marked with a ♡. Remember, when you want to do something about your weight, cut down on fat, *never* on potatoes!

Soups

"Whenever I fall in love, I begin with potatoes."

NORA EPHRON
Heartburn

RED PEPPER AND TOMATO BORSCHT WITH VEAL-POTATO BALLS ♡

A hearty, vividly flavored soup that is a rather wild improvisation on a very classic theme. It really is a stunning creation and makes a marvelous supper dish with some crusty bread.

"Some salt, some potatoes, and dried herbs, a few slugs of spirit and we become a very merry party."

MARTIN WALKER
The (London) Times, 1986

Makes 10 cups

2 large sweet onions, chopped
1 small carrot, peeled and chopped
1 medium baking potato, peeled and coarsely chopped
½ tablespoon butter or vegetable oil
6½ cups chicken or vegetable stock
8 large red bell peppers, trimmed, ribbed, seeded, and coarsely diced
Salt and freshly ground pepper
5 shallots, coarsely chopped
3 cloves garlic, chopped
Grated rind of half a small lemon
1 cup chopped sun-dried tomatoes
1 teaspoon red wine vinegar
1 cup red wine
½ teaspoon ground allspice
1 large can (1 pound, 12 ounces) plum tomatoes, drained and chopped
1 tablespoon golden raisins
1 tablespoon brown sugar
1 tablespoon lemon juice
1 heaping tablespoon tomato paste
1 tablespoon chopped fresh parsley
Purée from ½–1 large head roasted garlic (page 35)

1 small cabbage (8–10 ounces), cored,
    trimmed of tough outer leaves, and
    shredded (about 6 cups)
Veal-Potato Balls (page 39)
Sour cream or yogurt
Fresh dill

1. Combine the onions, carrot, potato, butter or oil, and ½ cup stock in a soup pot. Cover and bring to a boil. Reduce heat and simmer briskly for 3 to 4 minutes. Uncover and cook, stirring occasionally, until the liquid is gone and the vegetables are browning. Stir in the peppers.

2. Pour in the remaining stock. Season to taste with a bit of salt and pepper. Simmer, partially covered, for ½ hour, or until the vegetables are very tender. Set aside to cool.

3. While the soup is simmering, combine the shallots, garlic, lemon rind, sun-dried tomatoes, vinegar, and wine in a skillet. Cover and bring to a boil. Uncover and boil until the wine has evaporated. Cook, stirring, on moderate heat until the shallots are tender.

4. Remove from heat and add the allspice. Stir to coat the vegetables, then stir in the remaining ingredients except the cabbage. Simmer, uncovered, until thick, approximately 15 minutes.

5. Purée the cooled pepper mixture in the blender, in batches, and then push through a sieve. The pepper skins will be left behind. Discard them. Combine the sieved pepper mixture and the tomato mixture in the soup pot. Add the cabbage. Thin with more broth if necessary. Simmer, partially covered, for 20 minutes, until the cabbage is almost tender.

6. Add the Veal-Potato Balls. Simmer, partially covered, for 10 minutes to blend the flavors and finish the cabbage. Taste and adjust seasonings, adding more salt, pepper, lemon juice, and brown sugar as needed. The soup should have a nice balance of sweet and sour. If possible, refrigerate for a day or so to mellow.

7. To serve, heat until piping hot. Serve in shallow soup bowls garnished with dollops of sour cream or yogurt and dill.

"Potato; bland, amiable, and homely, an honest vegetable, giving honor where honor is due—to honest soup."

DELLA LUTES
The Country Kitchen

SPLIT PEA SOUP♡

This soup reaches ambrosial proportions if you use a stock made from ham hocks, or smoked chicken or turkey bones. Be sure to chill the stock and skim the fat before using it in the soup. Don't omit the garlic; it is the soul of this wonderful brew.

Makes approximately 4½ quarts

½ pound yellow split peas, rinsed and picked over
2 medium baking potatoes, peeled and cubed
10 cups chicken or vegetable stock
1 large onion, chopped
½ tablespoon butter or margarine
Purée from ½–1 head roasted garlic (page 35)
¼ cup grated Parmesan (optional)
Salt

1. Combine the peas, potatoes, and 6 cups stock in a saucepan. Bring to a boil, reduce heat, and simmer briskly, partially covered, for 40 to 50 minutes, or until the peas and potatoes are tender. Cool slightly.

2. While the vegetables are simmering, combine the onion and butter with ½ cup stock in a skillet. Cover and bring to a boil. Uncover, reduce heat, and simmer, stirring occasionally, for 10 minutes, or until the onions are browned and the stock has evaporated.

3. When the peas and potatoes are tender, purée in a blender and then push them through a fine sieve. Return the mixture to the pot. Add the sauteed onion and the remaining stock, then stir in the garlic purée.

4. Simmer the soup for approximately 15 minutes. If it seems too thick, add more stock as needed. Add the cheese and stir gently until it melts into the soup. Taste and add a touch of salt, if needed. Serve piping hot.

POTATO-TARRAGON SOUP

Don't substitute dried tarragon; it just isn't the same. The soup couldn't be simpler. It's a celebration of its ingredients.

Serves 4

2 tablespoons (¼ stick) butter
2 leeks, trimmed, cleaned, and sliced
4 cups chicken stock
1 pound baking potatoes, peeled and
    coarsely diced
Salt and pepper
½ tablespoon chopped fresh tarragon
2 tablespoons freshly grated Parmesan

1. Heat the butter in a heavy pot. Sauté the leeks until limp but not browned.

2. Add the stock, potatoes, and salt and pepper to taste. Simmer for 10 to 15 minutes, or until the potatoes are very tender. With a wooden spoon, crush some of the potatoes against the side of the pot.

3. Stir in the tarragon and cheese. Serve at once. Pass additional grated Parmesan at the table.

MR. POTATO HEAD

Mr. Potato Head, that venerable and beloved fellow, has been around for more than thirty-five years. In the early days, the toy consisted of a box of mixed facial parts (ears, nose, eyeballs) and a few accessories (hats, pipe, and so on). Today's effete children get a molded plastic potato as well, with slots for the various parts, but in the old days we had to supply the potato—a real one. All across the nation, mothers stalked through houses and apartments, inhaling deeply with a pained expression. "What is that appalling smell?" (Or stink, or odor—it depended on your mother.) Inevitably, the box of Mr. Potato Head parts would be hauled out, and there, with most of the pieces stuck into it, would be a beloved but withered and smelly spud. With exclamations of disgust, the tuber would be ditched, a fresh one dug out of the vegetable bin, and the Mr. Potato Head cycle would begin again. Mr. Potato Head co-exists with a Mrs. (handbag, earrings, big red lips). Mr. Potato Head lost his pipe in 1988, in keeping with today's climate of healthy living.

ROASTED ROOT VEGETABLE SOUP ♡

Some of the vegetables in this delicious vegetable stew tend to get short shrift from today's cooks. Parsnips, rutabagas, turnips—these roots make splendid eating, especially when combined with fennel and a mustard-tarragon–soy sauce base. To make a more substantial main-course soup, add sliced knockwurst in Step 6.

Makes 1¾ quarts

1 head garlic, each clove peeled
1 Spanish onion, cut in half, then into ½-inch wedges
1 bulb fennel, trimmed and cut into ½-inch wedges
1 small rutabaga, peeled and cut into ½-inch pieces
1 medium baking potato, unpeeled, cut into ½-inch pieces
1 large parsnip, peeled and cut into ½-inch pieces
2 carrots, peeled and cut into ½-inch slices
2 stalks celery, sliced into ½-inch pieces
1–2 tablespoons butter or margarine, in pieces
5 cups vegetable stock
½ cup plus 2–3 tablespoons red wine
½ teaspoon, crumbled tarragon
1 tablespoon Dijon mustard
2 tablespoons tomato paste
3–4 dashes soy sauce
Juice of ½ large lemon
1 piece Parmesan rind
Salt and freshly ground pepper to taste
1 can (14 ounces) white beans, drained and rinsed

1. Preheat the oven to 450°F.

2. Spread all the vegetables into a wide, shallow baking dish. Dot with butter and pour in ½ cup stock. Stir to combine everything very well. Bake, uncovered, for 30 minutes, shaking the pan occasionally.

3. Pour the 2 to 3 tablespoons of wine into the dish, and stir and scrape with a wooden spoon to dislodge the browned bits. Scrape the vegetables into a soup pot.

4. Pour in the remaining stock. In a small bowl, stir together the tarragon, mustard, tomato paste, soy sauce, lemon juice and ½ cup wine. Add the mixture to the soup, then add the Parmesan rind and season to taste.

5. Simmer, partially covered, for 15 minutes.

6. Stir in the beans. Taste and adjust seasoning. Simmer for 10 to 15 minutes more, until the ingredients are very tender. Taste and adjust seasonings.

CREAMY AND SPICY POTATO SOUP

This elegant and compelling soup is very creamy (although it contains no cream) and has a most attractive golden terra-cotta color. Although it contains plenty of garlic and spices, it tastes neither garlicky nor overly spicy. In England, I make this soup with Wilja Potatoes; an "all-purpose" cultivar that falls somewhere between floury and waxy, and imparts exactly the right creaminess to the finished dish. In the United States, the recipe was tested with round red potatoes, yielding a similar creaminess.

Makes approximately 2 quarts

1 head garlic
3 medium onions, halved and sliced into
    thin half-moons
1/3 cup chicken or vegetable stock
1 tablespoon butter
Salt and freshly ground pepper
2 tablespoons vegetable oil
2 tablespoons sesame seeds
1 tablespoon fennel seeds
1/2–1 teaspoon ground cumin
6 medium, round red or similar all-purpose
    potatoes, peeled and quartered
6 cups vegetable stock
1 large red bell pepper, coarsely chopped
1 pound frozen corn kernels
1 can (14 ounces) chopped Italian plum to-
    matoes
1 tablespoon fresh lime juice

1. Separate the head of garlic into cloves. Hit each clove lightly with a kitchen mallet to loosen the skin. Remove and discard the skin.

2. Spread the onions and garlic in a large, heavy frying pan. Pour in the stock and add butter. Season with a bit of salt and pepper. Cover and bring to a boil. Reduce heat and simmer briskly for 5 minutes. Uncover and cook over moderate heat, stirring occasionally; for 5 to 10 minutes, or until the onions are amber brown and the stock has cooked away.

3. Meanwhile, heat the oil in a soup pot. Stir in the seeds and cumin. Cook gently, stirring, for 2 to 3 minutes.

4. Add the potatoes. Stir and cook for 2 to 3 minutes more.

5. Stir in the onion mixture and the remaining ingredients. Simmer, partially covered, for 30 minutes, or until the potatoes are very tender. Cool.

6. Purée the mixture in batches in the blender, and push through a sieve. The soup may now be refrigerated for several days. To serve, reheat and adjust seasonings.

EASY CORN CHOWDER

This is a pantry soup, thrown together from things always on hand. It tastes as if a lot of time and effort have gone into it. The chowder is perfect for sipping out of sturdy pottery mugs, in front of the fire while snowbound.

Serves 2

2 slices bacon, diced
3 scallions, sliced
1 medium potato, cooked and diced (a good
    way to use up a leftover potato)
1 can (16 ounces) creamed corn
1 cup half-and-half or milk
Pinch of cayenne (ground red) pepper
Pinch of dried thyme
Pinch of grated nutmeg
Salt and freshly ground pepper

1. Cook the bacon and scallions together in a heavy pot for 3 to 5 minutes, or until the scallions are limp and the bacon is almost crisp. Add the potato. Cook for for 1 minute more, stirring occasionally.

2. Pour in the corn, half-and half, cayenne, thyme, nutmeg, and salt and pepper to taste. Simmer for 10 minutes. Serve at once.

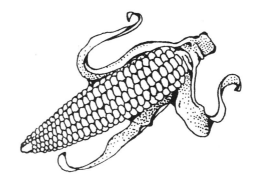

Mashed and Baked

"Excellent potatoes, smoking hot and accompanied by melted butter of the first quality, would alone stamp merit on any dinner."

THOMAS WALKER
The Original, 1935

THE REAL THING: MASHED AND BAKED

When all is said and done, freshly made mashed potatoes, prepared from good old Idaho Russets, are by far the best, although it takes some time. I have changed my method in recent years. No more boiling, steaming, draining, and so on. Simply bake large Idahos (pierce them first in several places with the tines of a fork) in a hot oven (450°F.) for at least 1½ hours. Baked potatoes make the most delectable mashed potatoes from both a taste and texture standpoint. Snatch the potatoes from the oven when they are done. Put the spuds on your work surface and with a fork, perforate them on top lengthwise and crosswise, then squeeze them open so that the potato flesh comes surging up. This is very important; do not be tempted to cut them open. The flesh of a cut potato will not have the floury, steamy, fluffy quality of a perforated and squeezed one. Scoop the potato flesh into a bowl and mash with an old-fashioned masher. You can put the potatoes through a ricer, if you wish, for a lighter and airier effect, but I prefer the homey quality of a masher. Always leave a lump or two to show that these are *real* mashed potatoes, but don't overdo the lumpiness or they will be awful. When they are mashed to your liking, use a wooden spoon or a mixer to beat in buttermilk and Parmesan.

MASHED POTATOES FOR SUPPER If you
are a potato purist, eat the potatoes piled into a bowl with no embellishment whatever. But it sometimes pays to abandon purity. For a simple and unbelievably comforting supper, for example, serve your gorgeous mashed spuds in a shallow soup bowl (use your nicest pottery; it will taste even better). Have ready bowls of garnishes, such as salsas, Red-Wine Mushrooms (page 29), or Browned Onions (page 31). Make a well in the mashed potatoes. Spoon some Browned Onions in the well and alternate dollops of salsa and Red-Wine Mushrooms around the edges. Grab a large spoon, settle into a comfortable chair, and eat blissfully.

MASHED POTATO VARIATIONS Add one of
the following vegetables to mashed potatoes (steam or bake the vegetables, and use equal portions of vegetables and potatoes): mashed rutabagas, mashed parsnips, mashed turnips, mashed carrots, or mashed celeriac. Or stir one of these into mashed potatoes: creamy goat cheese, chopped chives, an onion that has been baked until tender and then peeled and puréed, or purée of roasted garlic (page 35).

"If someone is given a salary for the preparation of mashed potatoes, how is it paid? In one lump sum."

SHAWM KREITZMAN

MASHED POTATOES

Mashed potatoes: Just whisper these two magic words into the still air, and the most troubled souls begin to unkink, relax, and drift into serene calm. Imagine the potatoes themselves, in hot, fluffy, creamy mounds piled into a warm bowl. Include a capacious, round soup spoon in your vision— just the thing to ferry soft dollops from bowl to mouth. Some fanatics insist on picturing the potatoes all alone. Why bother dreaming of gravy, roasts, stews, sausages? They believe that such inconsequential foodstuffs cannot match the perfection of the mashed spuds; they only diminish their glory.

The Quick Way: Mashed-potato addicts eat this soothing food often. A big breakfast bowlful of the stuff is not unheard of. When life's trials and tribulations are eased by generous and frequent helpings, a method of preparing mashed potatoes that is both quick and relatively low in calories is desperately needed. Here it is:

Search local speciality markets and natural foods stores for a brand of instant mashed potatoes called Barbara's Natural Mashed Potatoes. It's made from *unpeeled* Russet potatoes and tastes wonderfully unlike instant potatoes. To make 2 cups of mashed potatoes, measure 1½ cups of water into a heavy saucepan. Add salt to taste and a generous pinch each of ground cumin and cayenne (ground red) pepper. Bring just to a boil, then remove from the heat and stir in 1½ cups of the instant potatoes. Stir until smooth. Immediately stir in 1 cup of room-temperature buttermilk and several heaping tablespoons of grated Parmesan. Add more seasonings, buttermilk, or cheese to taste, and serve at once.

Quick Mashed Potato Salad: Not all potato salads are made with diced potatoes. Warm mashed potatoes beaten with garlicky vinaigrette and herbs are a perfect foil for steamed slices of cured tongue, corned beef, or warm smoked sausages.

Prepare instant mashed potatoes (see above), but substitute milk for the buttermilk and omit the cheese and spices. While the potatoes are still warm, beat in some well-seasoned, garlicky vinaigrette (try the Mustard Vinaigrette on page 85), chopped parsley, and sliced scallions or minced shallots. Serve warm or at room temperature.

POTATO PIZZA

The crust of this pie is soft and tender, much like the texture of potato gnocchi. Vary the topping with sautéed mushrooms, browned onions, or strips of roasted peppers. Potato Pizza makes a rustic and pleasing first course or light meal. The dough can be made ahead and refrigerated for a day. Day-old Potato Pizza reheats very well in the microwave.

Makes two 9-inch pies

1¼ pounds Idaho Russet potatoes, baked, scooped out of their shells, and mashed
1 cup all-purpose flour
Salt and freshly ground pepper to taste
Olive oil
1 can (1 pound, 12 ounces) plum tomatoes, drained
1 pound mozzarella, shredded
½ cup grated Parmesan
2 tablespoons shredded fresh basil, or ½ teaspoon dried

1. Preheat the oven to 400°F.

2. In a bowl, with your hands, mix the potatoes, flour, salt, and pepper to a smooth paste.

3. Oil two 9-inch pie pans with a bit of the olive oil. Divide the potato dough in half and spread half the dough ¼ inch thick on the bottom of one of the pans and up the sides. Sprinkle lightly with a little bit of oil. Repeat with the rest of the dough in the second pan.

4. Cut the tomatoes into strips and lay them on the potatoes. Sprinkle with the mozzarella, Parmesan, and basil. Sprinkle a touch more oil over all.

5. Bake for 20 to 30 minutes, or until bubbly and brown.

"There is said to be a transport cafe somewhere in the north (of England) which offers meat and two veg. The two veg being chips and potatoes."
MILES KINGTON
The (London) Times, 1986

PIPERADE POTATOES

A colorful and savory mixture of tomatoes, peppers, onions, and herbs are mixed with mashed potatoes and baked under a mantle of cheese. It smells good and tastes even better.

Serves 6

3 large onions, cut in half and sliced into paper-thin half-moons
1 teaspoon olive oil
Approximately ½ cup chicken or vegetable stock
3 large cloves garlic, crushed
3 large bell peppers, cut in half lengthwise, peeled, and sliced into thin strips (use 1 red, 1 green, 1 yellow, if possible)
1 can (1 pound, 12 ounces) tomatoes, well drained, seeded, and sliced into strips
¼ teaspoon crumbled dried oregano
¼ teaspoon crumbled dried basil
½ cup chopped fresh parsley
Salt and freshly ground pepper
4 large baking potatoes, baked
¼ cup grated Parmesan
¼ cup grated Gruyère

1. Combine the onions, oil, and ½ cup stock in a wide, heavy, nonreactive skillet. Cover and bring to a boil. Cook for 3 to 4 minutes, then uncover and turn the heat down. Simmer briskly for 5 to 7 minutes, or until the onions are tender and amber brown and the stock is just about gone. Use a little more stock if needed to scrape up the browned bits on the bottom of the pan.

2. Add the garlic and peppers. Cook, stirring occasionally, for 5 to 7 minutes, or until the peppers are tender. Stir in the tomatoes, dried herbs, and parsley. Simmer, uncovered, until thick and saucy. Season to taste with salt and pepper.

3. Preheat the oven to 400°F.

4. Perforate the potatoes and squeeze so the flesh surges up. Scoop into a bowl and mash well. Beat in the vegetable mixture. Taste and adjust seasoning, then spread in a shallow 9 x 13-inch baking dish. Sprinkle evenly with cheeses. (Save the potato skins for a special treat; see page 43.) Bake, uncovered, for ½ hour, until browned and bubbly.

POTATO GNOCCHI

Gnocchi are small, ineffably tender potato dumplings that are sauced and served like pasta. Gnocchi rate very high on the comfort food scale.

Serves 4 to 6

3 large baking potatoes
1½ cups all-purpose flour
2 teaspoons salt
2 tablespoons olive oil
2 eggs, lightly beaten
Additional flour for kneading
½ cup (1 stick) butter, melted and hot
Grated Parmesan or Chunky Tomato Sauce

**"Pray for peace and grace and spiritual food,
For wisdom and guidance, for all these are good
But don't forget the potatoes."**

JOHN TYLER PETTES

1. Boil the potatoes in their skins until thoroughly cooked. Cool slightly and peel.

2. Put the potatoes through a ricer. Measure 4 cups of riced potatoes into a large bowl. Add the flour and salt. Add the oil and toss with a fork. Add the eggs and stir until a sticky dough is formed.

3. Lightly flour your work surface. Turn out the dough and knead about 15 to 20 turns until smooth and pliable. Pull off a chunk of dough and roll it between your palms and on the floured surface into a rope a little thicker than your finger. Cut the rope into 1-inch pieces. If desired, dent each piece lightly with your finger or with the tines of a fork. Place the gnocchi on a floured baking sheet or platter. Repeat until all dough is used.

4. Bring a large quantity of salted water to a boil in a deep pot. Drop the gnocchi, a few at a time, into the boiling water and cook until they rise to the top. Have a baking dish waiting, with the melted butter in it. As the gnocchi rise to the surface, remove them with a skimmer or slotted spoon and mix with the butter in the baking dish. When all the gnocchi are cooked and mixed with the butter, serve at once, or cover tightly and keep warm in a very low oven for 1 to 2 hours. Serve sprinkled with grated cheese or serve Chunky Tomato Sauce. (Omit the butter if you use the tomato sauce.)

Chunky Tomato Sauce ♡

Serve this with gnocchi, or spooned into baked potatoes. If you love sun-dried tomatoes, as I do, add a handful, chopped, in Step 1.

Makes 4 cups

3 shallots, finely chopped
2 cloves garlic, peeled and crushed
Pinch of cayenne pepper
¾ cup chicken or vegetable stock
¾ cup red or white wine, or vermouth
½ tablespoon olive oil
1 tablespoon chopped fresh parsley
1 tablespoon each chopped fresh basil,
    thyme, and oregano; or ¼ teaspoon
    each dried
Salt and freshly ground pepper
3 cans (1 pound, 12 ounces each) plum to-
    matoes, drained and crushed
Pinch of sugar
1 piece Parmesan rind
2 tablespoons tomato paste

1. Combine the shallots, garlic, cayenne, stock, wine, oil, and herbs in a heavy skillet. Cover and bring to a boil, then boil for 5 minutes. Reduce heat, uncover, and simmer briskly until almost all the liquid has been evaporated and the onions are browned and tender.

2. Stir in the tomatoes (you can crush them with your hands), sugar, Parmesan rind, and salt and pepper to taste. Simmer, partially covered, for 15 minutes. Stir in the tomato paste and simmer for 5 minutes more, until thick and savory. Taste and adjust seasonings. Discard the Parmesan cheese rind.

PLAYING WITH YOUR FOOD

In certain rural parts of America, wrestling in gooey food is fast replacing football games and proms as a popular high-school extracurricular activity. Jell-O, chocolate pudding, creamed spinach, oatmeal, spaghetti—intrepid teenage wrestlers have wallowed in huge vats of all of these. But best of all, apparently, is mashed sweet potatoes. According to a Pennsylvania food-wrestling promoter, "There's quite an attraction. When you go down, you come up looking like a big orange monster."

MASHED POTATOES WITH MUSHROOMS AND LEEKS

This is one of those impossibly rich and decadent recipes to be indulged in when you want something special, and you've thrown calorific caution to the winds. The first taste is usually greeted by stunned silence, followed by compulsive gobbling. The sour cream separates very slightly, but it doesn't matter. This dish is pure luxury.

Serves 8 to 10

6 large baking potatoes
3 tablespoons butter
1 bunch leeks, trimmed, washed, and thinly sliced
2 pounds mushrooms, thinly sliced
1 tablespoon vegetable oil
Salt and pepper to taste
½ cup (1 stick) softened butter, cut into pieces
1 cup buttermilk
1 cup sour cream, at room temperature

1. Cook the potatoes in boiling, salted water to cover until tender.

2. Meanwhile, heat 1 tablespoon butter in a skillet, and cook the leeks for 5 to 7 minutes, until tender and golden. Set aside.

3. In a large skillet over moderate heat, cook the mushrooms in the remaining 2 tablespoons butter and 1 tablespoon oil, stirring frequently until they begin to render their juices. Turn up heat and continue cooking until they are almost dry. Season with salt and pepper, and set aside.

4. Preheat the oven to 350°F.

5. When potatoes are tender, drain, peel, and return them to the pot. Toss over low heat to dry, then put them through a ricer into a mixer bowl. Beat in the softened butter, buttermilk, and salt and pepper to taste.

6. Spread half the potatoes on the bottom of a shallow baking dish. Spread the mushrooms over the potatoes, and the leeks over the mushrooms. Spread with 1 cup sour cream and cover with remaining potatoes. (The dish can be made in advance and refrigerated at this point. Bring to room temperature before continuing.)

7. Bake, uncovered, for 45 minutes to 1 hour, or until browned and bubbling.

QUICK, LOW-CALORIE MASHED POTATO GRATIN ♡

1. Preheat the broiler.

2. Make quick mashed potatoes (page 23).

3. Split a garlic clove and rub the inside of a gratin dish with the split sides. Discard the garlic.

4. Spread the potatoes evenly in the dish. Drizzle a thin layer of skim milk over the potatoes. Sprinkle with Parmesan.

5. Bake under the broiler for 2 to 5 minutes, or until brown and puffy. Serve at once.

RED-WINE MUSHROOMS FOR MASHED POTATOES ♡

At first, there will seem to be too many mushrooms and not enough liquid, but soon enough the mushrooms release their juices and they seem swamped. Let them cook until most of the liquid is gone; they will be tender and richly flavored. Nothing brings out the taste of mushrooms like wine, stock, and soy sauce. Serious dieters can leave off the butter; you'll hardly miss it.

Makes approximately 1½ cups

1 pound large fresh mushrooms, halved and quartered
½ cup red wine
½ cup chicken or vegetable stock
Dash or 2 of soy sauce
½ tablespoon butter or margarine
Salt and freshly ground pepper

1. Combine the mushrooms, wine, stock, and soy sauce in a wide, heavy, nonreactive skillet. Add butter in pieces. Salt lightly.

2. Simmer, stirring frequently, for 10 minutes, or until the mushrooms are tender and most of the liquid has been absorbed. Season to taste. (These can be stored in the refrigerator and reheated when needed.) Serve with mashed potatoes.

ROASTED PEPPER AND TOMATO SALSA FOR MASHED POTATOES ♡

As far as I'm concerned, this is one of the best things you can serve with mashed potatoes. The icy coldness of the salsa, the steamy heat of the potatoes; the chunkiness and the smoothness, the spiciness and the blandness—these glorious contrasts make the combination a completely sensuous gastronomic experience.

Makes 1¼ cups

4 bell peppers (2 red and 2 yellow)
2 large cans (1 pound, 12 ounces each) plum tomatoes (substitute fresh tomatoes when "real" ones—juicy, ripe, flavorful—are in season)
Finely chopped fresh chiles to taste, or chopped canned chiles, or a mixture
2 cloves garlic, crushed
¼ cup red wine vinegar
2 tablespoons chopped fresh parsley
1 tablespoon chopped fresh coriander (optional)

1. Preheat the broiler. Line the broiler tray with foil, shiny side up. Place the peppers on the foil. Broil, turning frequently with tongs, until the peppers are charred on all sides. (This should take approximately 15 minutes.)

2. Place the peppers in a paper bag and close. Save any juices that have accumulated in the pan. After 10 minutes, remove the peppers. Pull out the cores and seeds and discard. Strip off the burnt skin and discard. Chop the peppers coarsely.

3. Drain the tomatoes and chop them. If fresh tomatoes are available, peel, seed, and juice them, then chop.

4. Combine all ingredients, including the peppers and pepper juices, in a nonreactive bowl. Chill.

BROWNED ONIONS FOR MASHED POTATOES

These onions are meltingly tender and caramelized to a beautiful amber brown. Make a big batch and store it in the refrigerator for mashed-potato evenings. The onions are also very good on hamburgers or with grilled skirt steak.

Makes about 2 cups

6 large onions, halved and sliced into thin
　　half-moons
1½ tablespoons butter, chicken or bacon fat,
　　or vegetable oil
2 cups rich chicken or vegetable stock
2–3 tablespoons dry white wine, vermouth,
　　or additional stock
Salt and freshly ground pepper

1. Combine the onions, butter, fat or oil, and stock in a heavy, deep skillet. Cover and bring to a boil. Reduce heat slightly and simmer briskly for 10 minutes.

2. Uncover. Simmer for approximately 35 to 40 minutes, stirring occasionally, until the onions are turning amber brown and the liquid is almost gone. Cook for a few more minutes, stirring constantly. The onions will begin to stick just a bit. Keep cooking and stirring for a few minutes more, using your wooden spoon to scrape up the browned deposits that form on the bottom of the skillet.

3. Turn the heat up a bit more and let the onions begin to burn. Not a disastrous scorching—just a little gentle burning and sticking on the bottom of the skillet. Splash in the wine or stock, and boil until it is just about evaporated, stirring and scraping up the browned bits vigorously. Season with salt and pepper to taste. Remove from the heat. Serve at once over mashed potatoes, or with a rubber spatula, scrape the lovely mass of browned onions into a bowl. Well covered, they will keep in the refrigerator for days.

HUNGARIAN ONIONS FOR MASHED POTATOES

Another enrichment for mashed potatoes: paprika-spiced onions and sour cream this time.

Makes approximately 1¼ cups

1 tablespoon butter or bacon fat
4 large onions, coarsely chopped
2 tablespoons Hungarian sweet paprika
Sour cream

1. Melt the butter in a skillet and toss in the onions. Cover and cook over low heat for 10 minutes. Uncover, raise heat a bit, and sauté for 10 to 12 minutes until golden.

2. Add the paprika. Stir over lowest heat for a minute or two, until the paprika has lost its raw taste.

3. Serve these with mashed potatoes along with a dollop of sour cream.

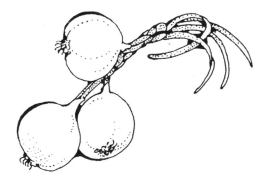

"He was a keen fellow; his whole life revolved around instant potatoes."
RICHARD EASSIC
In a speech at The Convenience Revolution, London, 1987

BRAISED SAUERKRAUT FOR MASHED POTATOES

At the end of a blustery Amsterdam day, spent walking next to the canals and popping into museums, I fell into a chair in the Rembrandt Café, exhausted, chilled, and ravenous. The proprietor rushed something he called *stampot* to the table: mashed potatoes and sauerkraut thoroughly mixed together, with sizzling sausages on the side. What a glorious combination! Try this braised sauerkraut mixed into your next bowl of mashed potatoes. A smoked sausage or two on the side, cooked until the flesh is almost bursting out of its crackling skin, certainly wouldn't hurt. And don't forget the mustard.

Makes 2 cups

1 large onion, halved and sliced into thin half-moons
2 cloves garlic, crushed (optional)
1 tablespoon butter
¼ cup dry white wine
Approximately 1½ cups chicken or vegetable stock
1 teaspoon crumbled dried thyme
1 pound sauerkraut, rinsed, drained, and squeezed dry (buy sauerkraut in a jar or a vacuum-packed bag, *never* in a can)
1 bay leaf
Salt and freshly ground pepper

1. Combine the onion, garlic, butter, wine, ½ cup stock, and thyme in a nonreactive, heavy skillet and simmer briskly for 10 minutes.

2. Uncover and cook, stirring occasionally, for 5 to 7 minutes, or until the onions are browned and tender. Stir in the sauerkraut, bay leaf, and enough remaining stock to barely cover the contents. Simmer, covered, for 30 to 40 minutes, stirring occasionally, until the sauerkraut is tender, lightly browned, and the liquid has been absorbed.

3. Discard the bay leaf and season to taste with salt and pepper. Serve mixed thoroughly into mashed potatoes.

MASHED POTATO GRATINS

Lovely gratins can be made with mashed potatoes. Let your imagination run wild in inventing variations. My favorite version contains sweet and mellow roasted garlic and onion as well as the mashed spuds. They can be wickedly indulgent or nicely low-calorie, as you wish.

LOW-CALORIE POTATO, ONION AND GARLIC GRATIN ♡

The baked vegetables give richness and deep flavor, and the milk and cheese bake into a gooey brown topping. Eat the gratin with pleasure and no guilt whatsoever.

Serves 6

4 large Idaho potatoes, baked, scooped out
    of their shells, and mashed
2 large heads roasted garlic (page 35)
2 large sweet onions, baked (see page 35)
Salt and freshly ground pepper
2–3 tablespoons buttermilk
4–5 tablespoons freshly grated Parmesan
¼ cup skim milk

1. Preheat the oven to 350°F.

2. Beat together the potatoes, garlic, onions, and salt and pepper to taste. Beat in the buttermilk.

3. Scrape the mixture into a gratin dish. Smooth the top and sprinkle with the cheese. (The recipe can be prepared in advance to this stage and refrigerated, covered, for a day or so. Bring to room temperature before proceeding.)

4. Drizzle the milk evenly over the top of the potatoes. Bake uncovered for 35 to 45 minutes, or until brown, bubbly, and thoroughly hot. Serve at once.

VARIATION Substitute baked mashed carrots, turnips, parsnips, or pumpkin for part of the potatoes.

MASHED-POTATO GRATIN WITH GARLIC AND ONIONS

Serves 6

2 large heads garlic
2 large sweet onions
4 large Idaho potatoes
1¼ cups heavy cream
Salt and freshly ground pepper
1 cup grated Gruyère

1. Preheat the oven to 425°F.

2. Remove the outer, papery covering of the garlic heads, but do not peel and do not separate the cloves. Well wrap the garlic heads in heavy-duty foil and put them in the oven. Put the onions on a double sheet of heavy-duty foil, but do not wrap them; put them in the oven. Pierce the potatoes in several places with a thin skewer or the tines of a fork. Put them directly on the oven rack. Bake the garlic for 1 hour and the onions and potatoes for 1¼ hours.

3. After 1 hour, pull out the package of garlic heads, unwrap, and let cool for 5 minutes. Separate the cloves and squeeze them over a bowl so that the softened garlic pops into the bowl.

4. After 1¼ hours, pull out the onions and potatoes. If the onions are not very soft (almost collapsed), put them back in for a few minutes. Perforate the potatoes lengthwise and crosswise with the tines of a fork and squeeze. Scoop the potato flesh into a bowl and mash it with a potato masher.

5. With a sharp knife, cut off the stem and root ends of the onions. Remove the skin and first layer. Put the onions in the container of a food processor and purée.

6. Combine the mashed potatoes, softened garlic, puréed onions, ¼ cup cream, and salt and pepper to taste in the bowl of an electric mixer, preferably fitted with a paddle attachment. Beat until smooth and blended, then scrape the mixture into a large gratin dish. Sprinkle the top with grated cheese. (The recipe can be prepared in advance to this point and refrigerated, covered, for a day or so. Bring to room temperature before proceeding.)

7. Reduce the oven temperature to 350°F. Pour the remaining cream over the mixture. Bake, uncovered, for 40 to 50 minutes, or until the top is browned and bubbly and the cream has cooked down to a very thick sauce-like consistency. Try to arrange to have some leftovers; this is very exciting when it's cold.

SANDY WILLIAMS'S TORTAS DE PAPA (POTATO CAKES)

Sandy Williams, my Latin American food advisor, says: "Tortas de Papa make a nice supper dish with salsa and a simple salad of romaine lettuce tossed with olive oil and salt. The potato cakes can be served with any sauce you prefer, but are especially good with a spicy sauce such as Salsa de Chipotle."

Makes 32 cakes

8 medium baking potatoes
Salt
½ cup crumbled feta cheese
2 eggs
3 tablespoons lard or vegetable oil
Salsa de Chipotle (recipe follows)

1. Boil the potatoes for 15 minutes or until well cooked; drain. When cool enough to handle but not cold, peel them. In a large bowl, mash them, add salt to taste and mix thoroughly. Set aside.

2. Using a pastry blender, coarsely chop the cheese. (Use an electric blender if you do not have a pastry blender.)

3. Combine the cheese and potatoes, mixing well using your fingers. Add the eggs and continue mixing by hand until the mixture is smooth. Taste and add salt if necessary.

4. Heat some of the lard in a frying pan over medium heat.

5. Scoop out a little bit of the potato mixture (about 2 tablespoons) and pat out a small cake with your fingers, flipping it gently from hand to hand until it is a uniform shape, about 3 inches in diameter and about ½ inch thick. Place potato cake in the hot lard and sauté for about 3 to 4 minutes. When the bottom edge is brown, flip it over to cook on the other side until also brown, another 3 to 4 minutes. Remove from the pan and drain it on paper towels. After patting out each cake, dip your fingers in a bowl of water so the next one will not stick to your fingers. Cook 3 or 4 cakes at once and add some lard to the frying pan after each batch.

6. Stack the drained potato cakes on a platter in a warm oven until ready to serve. (To store, wrap them in foil and refrigerate. Reheat by placing the foil package in a moderate oven for 15 to 20 minutes. They are not crisp on the outside when reheated, but still tasty.) Serve with Salsa de Chipotle.

Salsa de Chipotle

My friend, Sandy Williams, says, "Chipotle chiles are dried smoked jalapeños. They have a pungent flavor and give a dark, earthy color to anything prepared with them. Chipotle chiles are also sold in cans *en adobo,* a vinegar-based sauce, and can be substituted for dry chipotles. Salsa de Chipotle is served with Torta de Papa, eggs, beans, and plain meat dishes."

Makes approximately 1½ cups

8 chipotle chiles
2 ripe plum tomatoes

2 tomatillos, husks removed
1 clove garlic
¼ teaspoon salt
½ cup water

1. In a saucepan, boil the chiles for 20 to 30 minutes, until they are tender and puffed up. Drain and place in a blender jar. In another saucepan, boil the plum tomatoes and tomatillos in plenty of water for about 8 to 10 minutes, or until the tomatillos change to a dull green color. Drain and add to the chiles in the blender jar. Add garlic and salt, and blend well. Add water and blend again. Store covered in the refrigerator for a week or two. Serve cold.

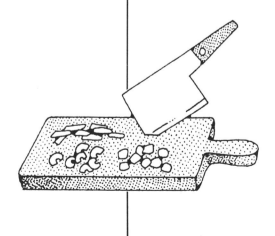

COLOMBIAN TOMATO CHEESE SAUCE FOR BAKED POTATOES

I tried very hard to track down a recipe for *Papas a la Huancaina* for this book. It is a Peruvian classic of cold boiled potatoes with white cheese and chili sauce. First, someone gave me a packet of instant Huancaina sauce: just add water and presto! a revolting mess. Then someone gave me a supposedly authentic Huancaina recipe that called for evaporated milk and a quantity of crushed saltines. Against my better judgment, I tried it and—what do you know? Another revolting mess. So I abandoned my quest for *Papas a la Huancaina* and concentrated on a different Latin American classic: *Papas Chorreades,* from Colombia. The meltingly creamy, spicy Chorreades sauce is traditionally served ladled over boiled potatoes. I like it spooned into large, freshly baked potatoes.

Makes 4 cups

2 cloves garlic, crushed
2 Spanish onions, chopped
½ tablespoon olive oil
½ cup chicken or vegetable stock
1–2 jalapeños, chopped
1 teaspoon turmeric
1 teaspoon ground cumin
1 can (1 pound, 12 ounces) tomatoes, drained and chopped
2 tablespoons chopped fresh coriander leaves
1½ cups shredded mozzarella
1 cup sour cream
Fresh coriander leaves

1. Combine the garlic, onions, oil, and stock in a skillet. Cover and boil for 3 to 4 minutes. Uncover, stir in jalapeños, reduce heat, and simmer for 5 to 7 minutes, until the onions are browned and tender and the stock has cooked away.

2. Stir in the turmeric and cumin. Stir over low heat for a minute or two, until the spices have lost their raw taste. Stir in the tomatoes.

3. Simmer, uncovered, for 20 to 25 minutes, until the mixture is thick.

4. Combine the mozzarella and sour cream.

Off the heat, stir the cheese mixture into the sauce. Return to the heat, stir, and cook over *lowest heat* just until melted into a creamy sauce containing soft little lumps of melted cheese. Try not to let the cheese get stringy. Remove from the heat at once and garnish with coriander leaves. Serve with perforated, squeezed open, freshly baked potatoes.

VEAL-POTATO BALLS

Mashed potatoes added to ground meat make exceptionally light and fluffy meatballs. Add these to the Red Pepper and Tomato Borscht (page 14), serve them with toothpicks on a buffet accompanied by a piquant dipping sauce, or toss them into pasta with a cream sauce scented with dill and allspice.

Makes approximately 50 meatballs

2 eggs
Grated rind of 1 small lemon
½ teaspoon dried dill
½ teaspoon ground allspice
Salt and freshly ground pepper to taste
1 pound ground veal
½ cup mashed potatoes
2 tablespoons chopped fresh parsley
½ tablespoon drained capers in vinegar, chopped
3 cloves garlic, minced

1. Beat the eggs with the lemon rind, dill, and allspice. Add to the veal with the remaining ingredients. Combine well with your hands. Fry a tiny piece in a small skillet and taste, then adjust seasonings to your liking.

2. Preheat the broiler. Line the broiler tray with foil, shiny side out. Lightly oil the broiler rack or spray it with vegetable spray.

3. Form the mixture into small balls smaller than walnuts but a little larger than marbles.

4. Place the meatballs 1 to 2 inches from the heat and broil for 2 minutes on one side and 3 minutes on the second side. Blot on paper towels.

MASSELLI'S SPECIAL

This is an old favorite of mine. Sausage-maker Paul Masselli—the Atlanta, Georgia, "Picasso of Pork Butts"—gave me the recipe years ago. Use the best Italian sausage you can find. You will need a large baking dish and the patience of a saint as the aroma of roasting sausages, potatoes, and vegetables fills your house.

Serves 6

Olive oil
1½ pounds Italian sausage links, mild or hot or combination of both, pricked with a fork
2 medium baking potatoes, peeled and quartered
2 medium sweet potatoes, peeled and quartered
2 large onions, peeled and very thinly sliced
2 large bell peppers (1 yellow, 1 red if possible), peeled and sliced
¼ cup water mixed with ¼ cup dry white wine
Salt and pepper

1. Preheat the oven to 350°F.

2. Lightly oil a large, shallow baking dish with olive oil. Place the sausage, potatoes, onions, and peppers in the dish. Pour the water and wine over all, and add salt and pepper to taste.

3. Bake, uncovered, for 1 to 1½ hours, turning the sausages occasionally until the sausages and potatoes are browned and cooked, and the onions have almost cooked down to a purée. If the baking pan becomes too dry at any time, add a bit more water and wine. Serve hot.

"Our greatest baking potato, of course, is the brown-skinned Idaho, which is grown in soil with a high lava content like the soil in Peru, where potatoes originated."

JAMES BEARD
The New James Beard

SHASHI'S PARMA ALOO

Shashi Rattan shared this unusual recipe, which has been in her family for years. I have substituted lemon juice for hard-to-find mango powder. Spiced and baked this way, the potatoes become tangy and irresistible morsels. Make plenty.

Makes 8 pieces

1 teaspoon vegetable oil
½ teaspoon turmeric
Pinch of cayenne pepper
½ teaspoon Garam Masala (recipe follows)
¼ teaspoon ground cumin
Juice of ½ small lemon
1 tablespoon tomato paste
8 small new potatoes

1. Preheat the oven to 350°F.

2. Combine all the ingredients except the potatoes in a bowl. Mix to a paste.

3. Peel the potatoes. Cut a ½-inch wedge out of each potato. Rub the space with spice paste and reinsert the wedge. Rub the potatoes all over with the remaining paste.

4. Place a rack on a baking tray and arrange the potatoes on the rack. Bake for 30 to 40 minutes, turning every 10 minutes, until tender. Serve at once as an appetizer or a snack.

Garam Masala

Makes about ¾ cup

¼ cup ground coriander
¼ cup ground cumin
1 tablespoon ground cinnamon
1 tablespoon ground cardamom
2 teaspoons black pepper
2 teaspoons ground cloves
2 teaspoons grated nutmeg
2 teaspoons ground ginger

Combine and then sift together. Store in an airtight jar.

"There's a whole world behind potatoes, but you must handle them gently and learn to understand their different flavors, textures and cooking qualities."
Gary Ely, produce buyer for English Safeway Stores, quoted in *The Sunday London Times*, January 1988

BEET PURÉE

One of the classic delights of Russian Jewish cooking is a cold, creamy bowlful of beet borscht served with a steamy-hot boiled potato floating in its center. If you split a hot baked potato and fill it with tangy beet purée, you reverse the classic. You can imagine the color, taste, and texture—what a terrific reversal!

Makes 1½ cups

2 pounds fresh beets
½ cup sour cream
1–2 cloves garlic, crushed
Salt and freshly ground pepper to taste
1½ tablespoons wine vinegar

1. Preheat the oven to 400°F.

2. Trim the greens away, if any; scrub the beets and wrap each one in heavy-duty foil, shiny side in. Bake for 1 to 2 hours, or until tender. (The timing depends on the age and size of the beets.) Use a skewer to test for doneness; the skewer should go in easily but the beets should not be mushy. Cool.

3. Trim the stem and root ends of the beets and slip off the skins. Cut beets into chunks and put in the bowl of a food processor with the remaining ingredients. Process to a rough purée, then taste and adjust the seasonings. It should be quite peppery, with a good balance of sweet and sour. Chill. The purée will keep in the refrigerator for a week or more.

"That which was heretofore reckon'd a food fit only for Irishmen and clowns is now become the diet of the most luxuriously polite."

STEPHEN SWITZER
Writing on Potatoes, 1733

POTATO SKINS ♡

For years, people ate the potatoes and threw away the peels. Now, I fear, in their zeal for potato-skin extravaganzas, they may be doing just the opposite. Don't succumb to either profligate practice. The skins are spectacular, baked until very crisp, but the flesh is equally spectacular baked in a gratin. Or try the scraps in Potato-Tarragon Soup (page 17).

Large baking potatoes

1. Preheat the oven to 400°F.

2. Scrub the potatoes, then halve them lengthwise.

3. With a teaspoon or a melonballer, scoop out the insides, leaving a shell about ¼ inch thick. Save the trimmings for another use (see Note). Bake directly on the oven rack for 25 to 35 minutes, or until golden brown and very crisp. Serve at once, as is; with dips; or filled with sour cream, chili, crumbled bacon and chives; or whatever you like.

Note Don't you dare throw the potato scraps away! Use them to make the wonderful gratin on the next page. It may be made at once, refrigerated, and reheated at a later date.

POTATO SKIN TREAT

When you bake potatoes and then scoop out the flesh for mashed potatoes or a gratin, Never Throw the Skins Away! Save them in the refrigerator. When you want a delectable treat, cut them into strips and lay them, skin side down, on a baking tray. Sprinkle with grated Parmesan or Gruyère, and drizzle (if you wish) with a bit of olive oil or clarified butter. Broil briefly or bake at 450°F. for 15 minutes or so, until the cheese is melted and the skins are crisp. Serve hot.

POTATO SCRAP GRATIN ♡

1. Scoop out the raw potato right into a saucepan and add enough chicken or vegetable stock to barely cover. Season with a bit of salt and plenty of pepper. If you wish, add a bit of nutmeg or a pinch of cumin and cayenne (ground red) pepper. Simmer, covered, for about 10 minutes, or until tender. Do not drain.

2. Mash roughly, right in the pot, with a potato masher; you don't want a purée, just a sort of roughly chopped effect. Spread mixture in a gratin dish. Drizzle on a bit of milk and sprinkle with some Parmesan. Bake, uncovered, for 50 to 60 minutes, or until bubbly and well browned on top.

"Why are potatoes so afraid of Indians? They don't want to get scalloped."

PAUL MCMAHON
Potato Jokes

BAKED POTATOES

I've always questioned the wisdom of pairing steak with baked potatoes. A properly baked spud is an exquisite thing; steak just gets in the way. One of the best suppers in the world is a basket of perfect, freshly baked potatoes and a selection of garnishes. All the mashed-potato enrichments—Hungarian Onions (page 32), Browned Onions (page 31), Red-Wine Mushrooms (page 29), salsa, buttermilk, Parmesan, and so on— are perfect for baked potatoes, too. Or try duxelles (chopped, sautéed mushrooms) folded into sieved cottage cheese, Dijon mustard stirred into yogurt, guacamole, or chutney.

To bake the perfect potato, choose a large Idaho Russet. Wash, scrub, and dry it; pierce in several places with a slim skewer; and bake directly on the oven rack at 425°F., for *at least* 1¼ hours. Longer is better—the skin gets crunchier and the flesh gets creamier. Perforate the potato on top lengthwise and crosswise, then squeeze so the floury, steamy flesh comes surging up. On consideration, forget the embellishments. Add just a shower of freshly ground pepper or a hint of fresh lemon juice. The contrast of crunchy skin and fluffy flesh and the deep potato taste are sheer bliss.

Gratins

"Potatoes no longer wear their jackets but arrive pale and naked in an impenetrable plastic bag."

FRANK MUIR
*An Irreverent and Thoroughly Incomplete
Social History of Almost Everything*

PIE FOR A MEXICAN SHEPHERD

Not at all authentic by either traditional or Mexican standards, this shepherd's pie is so delicious that authenticity doesn't matter at all. Last year, I had a complete turkey revulsion, and served this pie for Thanksgiving. It was such a hit that I may never roast another turkey.

Serves 8

1 pound lean ground chuck
1 pound lean ground pork
2 large onions, coarsely chopped
3 cloves garlic, minced
1 teaspoon ground cumin
1 tablespoon crumbled dried oregano
¼ teaspoon ground cinnamon
1 teaspoon hot red pepper flakes
Salt and freshly ground pepper to taste
1 can (16 ounces) tomato purée
5 large baking potatoes, freshly baked
1 large head roasted garlic (page 35)
1 cup buttermilk
¼ teaspoon cayenne pepper
1 cup grated Monterey Jack
1 cup grated longhorn cheddar
½ cup grated Parmesan
Fresh coriander (optional)

1. Combine the meats, onions, and garlic in a heavy, wide, nonreactive skillet. Brown over moderate heat for 5 to 7 minutes, breaking up the lumps with a wooden spoon as the meat cooks. When the meat is browned and the onions are limp, pour the mixture in a colander set over a bowl and let *all* the fat drain away. Discard the fat.

2. Return the meat mixture to the skillet and add ½ teaspoon cumin and the remaining spices. Stir over low heat until the meat is coated with the spices and they have lost their raw taste.

3. Stir in the tomato purée. Simmer gently for approximately 15 minutes, until it is absorbed. Cool somewhat.

4. Meanwhile, prepare the potatoes. Perforate them lengthwise and crosswise with a fork, and squeeze so that the potato flesh surges up. Scoop it into a bowl. Squeeze the pulp from the garlic and add it to the potato. Mash until perfectly smooth, then beat in the buttermilk, cayenne, remaining ½ teaspoon cumin, and salt and pepper to taste. (Save the potato skins for a private nibble.) Taste and add more seasonings if necessary.

5. Preheat the oven to 400°F.

6. Stir the Monterey Jack and cheddar into the cooled meat mixture. Spread it in a 9 × 13-inch baking dish. Beat half the Parmesan into the potatoes, then spread the potatoes over the meat. Sprinkle evenly with the remaining Parmesan. (If you wish, make the dish ahead to this point and store in the refrigerator. Bring to room temperature before continuing.) Bake, uncovered, for 50 to 60 minutes, or until puffy, browned, and bubbly. Garnish with the coriander and serve at once.

GRATIN OF VEGETABLES

This is a sort of ratatouille, with turnips and potatoes substituting for eggplant.

Serves 6

1 tablespoon olive oil
2 medium onions, cut in half and sliced into paper-thin half-moons
1 small red pepper, halved, peeled, and sliced
1 small yellow pepper, halved, peeled, and sliced
1 small green pepper, halved, peeled, and sliced
3 cloves garlic, crushed
3 small turnips, peeled and coarsely diced
3 small waxy potatoes, coarsely diced
1 can (14 ounces) plum tomatoes, drained and cut into strips
3 ripe tomatoes, peeled, seeded, juiced, and chopped (or substitute canned)
Salt and freshly ground pepper
3 tablespoons shredded fresh basil, or ¼ teaspoon crumbled dried
½ cup grated Gruyère

1. Heat the oil in a deep, heavy skillet. Sauté the onions over medium heat for 3 to 5 minutes, or until softened.

2. Stir in the peppers and garlic. Cook for a few minutes until the peppers lose their crispness.

3. Stir in the turnips, potatoes, tomatoes, and seasonings. Cover and simmer very gently for 15 to 20 minutes, or until the turnips and potatoes are tender. Spread the mixture in a gratin dish and sprinkle the surface with the cheese. (At this point the dish may be refrigerated until serving time, for a day or two if necessary.)

4. Preheat the oven to 350°F.

5. Bake, uncovered, for about 20 minutes, or until bubbling and lightly browned on top.

SHEPHERD'S PIE WITH RED LENTILS ♡

Another entry into the shepherd's pie stakes, this one is made with red lentils and a beautiful spice combination. Interesting shepherd's pies such as this one and the others in this collection make memorable party main dishes that fill guests with joy.

Serves 8

1 large Spanish onion, chopped
3 cloves garlic, minced
2 medium carrots, peeled and diced
1 yellow bell pepper, peeled and diced
1½ cups red wine
1½ cups chicken or vegetable stock, approximately
1 tablespoon butter
½ teaspoon each dried tarragon and thyme
¼ teaspoon each ground allspice and cinnamon
Pinch or 2 of cayenne pepper
3 tablespoons tomato paste
1 tablespoon golden raisins, soaked in ¼ cup red wine
½ cup split red lentils, washed, drained, and picked over
1 pound lean ground lamb, sautéed until brown and drained of fat.
Salt and freshly ground pepper
5 large baking potatoes, baked and mashed with 1 cup buttermilk
Generous pinch of ground allspice
6 tablespoons grated Parmesan

1. Spread the onion, garlic, carrots, and pepper in a large, heavy, nonreactive pan. Add 6 tablespoons red wine, ½ cup stock, and the butter in pieces. Cover and boil for 5 minutes. Reduce the heat and simmer gently for 5 to 10 minutes, stirring occasionally, until the carrots begin to get tender.

2. Stir in the herbs, spices, tomato paste, raisins and wine, lentils, lamb, and salt and pepper to taste. Stir in remaining 1 cup of stock. Cover and simmer for 20 minutes, uncovering to stir occasionally. If mixture gets too dry and threatens to stick, add a bit more stock.

3. After 20 minutes, uncover and cook for 5 to 10 minutes more, until the lentils are tender but not mushy, and still hold their shape; the mixture should be very thick.

4. Spread the lamb and lentil mixture in a gratin pan. Season the potatoes with allspice, a pinch of cayenne pepper, and salt. Spread over the meat mixture, and sprinkle evenly with Parmesan. (At this point the pie can be covered tightly with plastic wrap and refrigerated for 2 days. Bring to room temperature before proceeding.)

5. Preheat the oven to 375°F.

6. Bake the pie uncovered for 45 to 55 minutes, or until browned, puffed, and bubbly. Serve at once.

SHEPHERD'S PIE

If you think there are no gastronomic rewards for an American expatriate living in the English countryside, consider shepherd's pie. Like any simple dish, it can be quite appallingly bad, but when made properly, it's splendid.

To make a basic shepherd's pie, sauté lean ground lamb with chopped onions and carrots, adding a touch of Worcestershire sauce and a dab or two of tomato paste when the meat and vegetables are cooked. (Some people begin with leftover minced roast lamb.) Season the mixture well and spread in a gratin dish. Blanket it with a rich and thick layer of mashed potatoes, sprinkle with grated cheddar, and bake in a hot oven until bubbly, golden, and unbearably fragrant. Who can resist such splendid and simple fare?

The most fun, though, is fiddling with this basic formula. Englishmen and women frown at the crazy foreign cook, mucking up good food with added ingredients (ground cumin, for instance, or *garlic!*), but many of them, when offered a serving, scrape their plates clean and actually ask for seconds. I'm not sure they would admit it, however, if subsequently questioned.

CURRIED SHEPHERD'S PIE ♡

The list of ingredients may look daunting, but don't worry. You will be making your own curry powder, and a number of the ingredients are the spices needed for that. This is an extraordinary recipe; the meat-eggplant mixture is hot, sour, and sweet, and the potatoes are creamy with the mellow flavor of roasted garlic.

Serves 8

2 large Spanish onions, coarsely chopped
1¼ cups chicken or vegetable stock
½ tablespoon butter or margarine
1 teaspoon turmeric
1 teaspoon ground cumin
1 teaspoon pure chili powder
1 teaspoon ground coriander
1 teaspoon ground cardamom
¼ teaspoon ground ginger
¼ teaspoon dry mustard
¼ teaspoon ground cinnamon
¼ teaspoon cayenne pepper
Pinch of ground cloves and allspice
Pinch of grated nutmeg
Salt and freshly ground pepper to taste
3 cloves garlic, minced
1 pound lean ground lamb or beef
2 eggplants (½ to ¾ pound each), roasted, peeled and chopped (see Note)
1 can (14 ounces) tomatoes

½ cup raisins
¼ cup mango chutney
1 tablespoon fresh lemon juice
1 tablespoon Worcestershire sauce
8 dried apricot halves, minced (use scissors)
1 tablespoon tomato paste
7 large baking potatoes, baked and mashed with 1¼ cups buttermilk
½ teaspoon Garam Masala (page 41)
Purée from 1 head roasted garlic (page 35)

1. Spread the onions in a heavy frying pan. Adding *no* liquid or fat, heat the frying pan gently, then cook over moderate heat, without stirring, for 7 to 10 minutes, or until the onions are sizzling, speckled with dark amber, and beginning to stick to the pan.

2. Stir in the stock and butter in pieces, and let it bubble up, stirring up the browned deposits in the pan as it bubbles. Stir in all the spices and the garlic. Turn down the heat and simmer, stirring frequently, for 7 to 10 minutes, until the mixture is very thick (not at all soupy) and the onions and spices are frying in the butter and their own juices. Don't rush this step; it is essential that the spices do not have a harsh, raw taste. Taste. Cook gently for a few more minutes if necessary, then scrape the mixture into a bowl.

3. In the same skillet, cook the meat over medium heat for 5 to 7 minutes. As it browns, break up any lumps with a wooden spoon. When it is thoroughly cooked, drain in a colander set over a bowl. Discard the drained fat. Put the lamb and onion mixture back into the frying pan.

4. Stir in the eggplant, tomatoes, raisins, chutney, lemon juice, Worcestershire sauce, and apricots. Simmer, uncovered, for ½ hour, stirring occasionally. Stir in the tomato paste and simmer for 5 to 10 minutes more, until thick. Taste and adjust seasonings. Spread the mixture in a gratin pan.

5. Preheat the oven to 375°F.

6. Season the potatoes with cayenne pepper, Garam Masala, garlic purée, and salt and pepper. Taste and add more seasoning if needed. Spread the potatoes over the meat. (Make ahead to this point if you wish, and refrigerate. Bring to room temperature before continuing.)

7. Bake for 40 to 50 minutes, or until brown and bubbling.

Note To roast eggplants, preheat the oven to 400°F. Prick the eggplants in several places with a fork. Roast directly on the oven shelf for 40 to 60 minutes, or until soft and collapsed. Cool. (Eggplants can be roasted several days ahead of time and stored whole in the refrigerator.)

POTATO-LEEK CUSTARD

Potatoes and leeks go together like Bogart and Bacall. Here, they nestle in an unctuous cheese custard.

Serves 6

2½ pounds boiling potatoes
3 tablespoons butter
6 leeks, trimmed, cleaned, and thinly sliced
2½ cups grated Swiss (Gruyère, Emmentaler or a mixture)
1½ cups milk
Salt and pepper
Grated nutmeg
3 eggs

1. Steam the potatoes over boiling water for 10 minutes, or until tender but not mushy.

Cool and peel. Slice thinly.

2. Meanwhile, melt the butter in a wide, heavy skillet. Sauté the leeks in hot butter for 5 minutes, or until tender.

3. Preheat the oven to 375°F.

4. Butter a 2-quart baking dish. Layer the potatoes, then the leeks, then 2 cups of the cheese. Continue layering, ending with a top layer of potatoes.

5. Beat the milk with salt, pepper, and nutmeg to taste into the eggs. Pour over the potatoes. Cover with the remaining ½ cup cheese.

6. Bake, uncovered, for 30 to 40 minutes, or until the custard is set and the top is nicely browned.

SINFULLY RICH GRATIN OF POTATOES AND CHEESE

Another indulgence, this time it's sliced potatoes drowned in garlic-haunted cream and baked until the potatoes are meltingly tender and the cream becomes a sublime sauce. I wish I could eat this every day or even every week, but if I did, I'd be a blimp. Save the gratin for very special occasions, romantic or otherwise, unless you're one of those lucky and irritating people who can eat what they want without gaining an ounce.

Serves 8

2 large cloves garlic, peeled and flattened
4 large Idaho potatoes, sliced paper-thin
    (slice at the last minute so they don't
    darken; do not soak in cold water)
Salt and pepper
2 cups grated Gruyère
1 quart heavy cream

1. Preheat the oven to 325°F.

2. Rub the bottom and sides of a gratin dish with garlic. You can leave the garlic in the dish or discard it, depending on your passion for the glorious bulb.

3. Cover the garlic with a layer of the potatoes. Sprinkle on some salt and pepper to taste and the cheese. Pour some cream over the whole thing. Repeat until all the potatoes, cheese, and cream are used. With a spatula, press the top layer of potatoes into the cream.

4. Place the pan, uncovered, in the oven. (Put a baking sheet underneath to catch spills.) Bake for 1½ hours or more, until the top is browned, the potatoes are meltingly tender, and the cream has cooked down to a thick sauce.

Note This dish is as good at room temperature as it is hot; it makes a sensational picnic dish.

POTATO GRATIN VARIATIONS Potato gratins or old-fashioned scalloped potatoes—layers of sliced potatoes baked with savory ingredients—are delicious, filling, and infinitely variable. The gratin recipes represent the two ends of the potato-gratin spectrum: outrageously fattening (but ravishing) and incredibly noncalorific (almost equally ravishing). Either version can be used for these variations.

Potatoes Lyonnaise Layer some Browned Onions (page 31) between the potato layers. For the lower-calorie version, use just a dab of butter with a combination of stock and wine to brown the onions.

Potato and Mixed Mushroom Gratin Layer trimmed, sliced, shiitake, cultivated, and oyster mushrooms that have been simmered until tender and almost dry in a combination of stock, dry sherry, a dash or two of soy sauce, and a dab of butter. To make this a Lucullan dish, add some soaked, drained dried cèpes (porcini), and mix some of the filtered, drained soaking liquid in with the cream or stock.

Potatoes Roquefort Crumble some Roquefort cheese between the potato layers.

Main-Dish Gratin Layer some chopped ham (prosciutto is lovely) or some sliced smoked sausage.

Herbed Gratins Toss the potatoes with chopped fresh tarragon, thyme, and parsley, or with chopped rosemary.

Note Use only floury baking potatoes for your gratins. They soak up the liquid and seasonings in a most delightful way. Don't bother peeling the potatoes; you will increase the nutrition and lessen preparation time. Never soak the potato slices in water, or they will lose their starchiness (along with precious vitamins) and will not reach the proper degree of meltingness. Slice the potatoes just before you are about to use them.

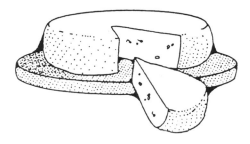

"The most successful diets so far seem to be:

A—Potatoes and Buttermilk.
B—Grass.
C—Bread and Butter.
D—Nine pounds of Horseflesh a day."
GEORGE BERNARD SHAW
In a Postcard to Mrs. Eileen Coghlin, 1940

HEAVENLY POTATO GRATIN

If you must use a canned stock here, add no additional salt. And choose your brand carefully; some are far too salty. With a good stock, this gratin, in its own way, is as delicious as the previous, wickedly indulgent one. The potatoes become exquisitely tender, the stock and cheese form a savory sauce, and you can eat *large portions* as often as you like, without fear of blimphood.

Serves 6 to 8

1 large clove garlic
4 large baking potatoes
¼ cup fresh grated Parmesan
Salt and freshly ground pepper
1½ cups excellent-quality homemade un-
    salted vegetable or chicken stock

1. Preheat the oven to 400°F.

2. Peel the garlic and split it. Rub a 9 × 13-inch oval gratin dish with the split sides of the garlic. Leave the garlic in the dish, if desired.

3. Slice the potatoes paper-thin. Do not soak them in water at any time.

4. Layer one-third of the potato slices in the gratin dish and sprinkle evenly with Parmesan and salt and pepper to taste. Pour one-third of the stock over the potatoes.

5. Repeat 2 more times. With a broad spatula, press the top layer down into the liquid.

6. Bake for approximately 1½ hours, or until the potatoes are tender, the liquid has cooked down to a thick sauce, and the top is brown and crusty.

"We being on land, the people came down to us on the water side with shew of great curtesie, bringing to us potatoes, rootes, and two very fat sheep."

The Journal of Sir Francis Drake, 1577

CHÈVRE POTATOES

Potatoes and goat cheese *put together!* Who could ask for anything more? Personally, I feel that this dish feeds two at most, but you may be able to exercise a bit more restraint.

Serves 4 to 6

5 ounces creamy goat cheese (chèvre), such
    as Montrachet
1¼ cups warm chicken stock
4 large baking potatoes, sliced ¼ inch thick
    (slice just before using; do not soak in
    water)
Salt and freshly ground pepper
1 clove garlic, split

1. Preheat the oven to 425°F.

2. Beat together the cheese and stock. Toss in a large bowl with the potato slices and salt and pepper to taste. Everything should be well combined.

3. Rub a gratin dish with the cut sides of the garlic. Leave the garlic in the dish if desired. Spread the potato mixture in the dish. Cover tightly with foil. Bake for 30 to 40 minutes, or until the potatoes are very tender and the sauce is thick and creamy. Stir the contents of the dish thoroughly halfway through the baking time.

"Everyone complained constantly about the food. My husband said it cost too much, Laurie said that there was not enough variety, Jannie said that we did not have mashed potatoes half often enough."

SHIRLEY JACKSON
Raising Demons

CAULIFLOWER-POTATOES MORNAY

Mornay sauce is considered very un-chic these days. Indeed, in some circles, it is positively shunned as hopelessly out of date and even unhealthy. Nonsense! A little flour never hurt anyone, and the sauce, when properly made, is indescribably smooth, soothing, and delicious. This combination of sauce with potatoes and cauliflower is a very special classic that does not deserve to be forgotten.

Serves 6 to 8

Sauce (Makes 2 cups)
1 cup dry or medium-dry sherry
4 tablespoons (½ stick) butter
3 tablespoons finely chopped shallots or scallions
¼ cup all-purpose flour
2 cups half-and-half, scalded
Salt and pepper
Pinch of grated nutmeg and cayenne pepper
3 tablespoons grated Gruyère

Vegetables
1 large cauliflower, trimmed and broken into large flowerets
1 pound new potatoes

Assembly
1 cup grated Swiss (Gruyère, Emmentaler, or a mixture)
¼ cup dry, whole-wheat bread crumbs
Pinch of cayenne (ground red pepper)

1. Make the sauce. Pour the sherry into a saucepan, and bring to a boil (stand back, in case the sherry flames.) Reduce the heat a bit and simmer briskly until reduced by half. Set aside.

2. In a heavy saucepan, melt the butter and sauté the shallots or scallions. Whisk in the flour and cook, stirring over medium heat, for about 3 minutes, or until the roux is a light golden color.

3. Whisk the hot sherry into the roux. The mixture will be quite thick. Whisk in the scalded half-and-half, then add salt and pepper to taste, nutmeg, and cayenne. Bring to a simmer and simmer slowly for 10 minutes or so, until smooth and thickened. Stir frequently with your wire whisk.

4. Remove from the heat and gently fold in the grated cheese, using a rubber spatula. Taste for seasoning and adjust if necessary. Set sauce aside until needed, covering with a piece of plastic wrap pressed against the surface to prevent a skin from forming. (The sauce may be refrigerated for use on the following day. It will thicken up quite a bit; thin by whisking in milk.)

5. Prepare the vegetables. Steam the cauliflower and potatoes (unpeeled) separately, until tender but not at all mushy. Cut each potato in half if large. The potatoes and flowerets should be approximately the same size.

6. Preheat the oven to 375°F. Thin the sauce if necessary, and heat very gently until just barely warm.

7. Place the cauliflower, potatoes, and sauce in a bowl and fold together. Spread mixture in a 9 × 13-inch gratin dish. Sprinkle with the cheese and bread crumbs, then add a tiny dusting of cayenne.

8. Bake, uncovered, for 30 minutes, or until browned and bubbly. Serve at once.

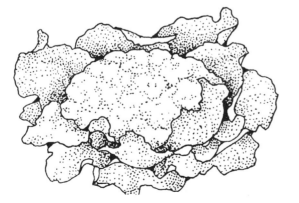

EDITORIAL SPECIAL

My editor, Harriet Bell, a woman of obvious taste and discernment, sent me her favorite comfort potato recipe. Here it is in her words:

"Yesterday was one of those cold, rainy Sundays when you are chilled to the bone from the minute you get out of bed. At 5:00 P.M., I put two medium Idahos in the toaster oven (for some reason, my electric toaster oven does a better job than my gas oven—it must have something to do with the circulation). Fifty minutes later, I took them out, split them open, and added to each one a small pat of butter, a few tablespoons of cottage cheese, and a couple of grinds of the peppermill. Heaven. Absolute heaven. The best part is tossing around the hot potato and cold cottage cheese with my tongue like a juggler so I never burn my mouth. My sweet little Romanian *bubbe* used to make this for me. What really galls me is to see someone ruin a perfectly good baked potato with something like caviar. Some people have no taste."

Casseroles

"What I say is that, if a man really likes potatoes, he must be a *pretty decent sort of fellow.*"

A. A. MILNE
Not That It Matters

KEEMA CURRY WITH POTATOES ♡

Keema Curry is a homestyle dish, a sort of East Indian chile con carne. It is often cooked with peas, but the best version has potatoes stirred into the spicy ground lamb.

Serves 6

2 medium onions, cut into eighths
½ tablespoon clarified butter or margarine
2½ cups chicken or vegetable stock
2 teaspoons minced, peeled fresh ginger
2 cloves garlic, minced
1 teaspoon ground cinnamon
1 teaspoon ground coriander
Pinch of ground cloves
½ teaspoon ground allspice
6 whole green cardamom pods, lightly
    crushed
1 dried bay leaf, broken in half
Salt and freshly ground pepper to taste
1 green chile, stemmed, seeded, and minced
2 medium boiling potatoes, cut into 1-inch
    dice
3 tablespoons tomato paste
1½ pounds lean ground lamb
1 can (12 ounces) chopped tomatoes
1 teaspoon Garam Masala (page 41)

1. Separate the segments of the onion pieces and spread them in a large, heavy, nonstick frying pan. Add *no* liquid or fat and heat the frying pan gently. Cook over moderate heat, without stirring, for 7 to 10 minutes, or until the onions are sizzling, speckled with dark amber, and beginning to stick to the pan.

2. Stir in the butter and 1 cup of stock, and let it bubble up, stirring up the browned deposits in the pan with a wooden spoon as it bubbles. Stir in the ginger, garlic, spices, and chile. Turn the heat down a bit and simmer, stirring frequently, for 5 to 7 minutes, until the mixture is very thick (not at all soupy) and the onions and spices are frying in the butter and their own juices. Don't rush this step; it is essential that the spices not have a raw, harsh taste. Taste, and cook very gently for a few more minutes if necessary.

3. Toss the potatoes in the spice mixture until well coated. Stir in the tomato paste.

4. In another frying pan, cook the meat for 5 to 7 minutes, until it loses its red color. Break it up with a wooden spoon as it cooks. Drain well in a colander set in a bowl. Discard the drained fat. Stir the meat into the onion-potato mixture.

5. Stir in the remaining stock and the tomatoes. Bring to a boil. Reduce the heat and simmer briskly for about 30 minutes, uncovered, until the mixture is thick. Cover and simmer for 15 minutes more, or until the potatoes are done. If at any time the mixture threatens to stick and burn, stir in a bit more stock. Stir in the Garam Masala and serve at once. (Or cool, cover, and refrigerate for a day or so.) Serve with Basmati rice and yogurt mixed with chopped fresh mint.

LESCO POTATOES

It's hard to believe that potatoes, tomatoes, and paprika—those essentials of Hungarian cooking—were gifts of the New World and didn't hit Hungary until the Turks invaded, which is not all that long ago in historic terms. The Magyars knew nothing about such ingredients. This soul-warming potato stew makes excellent use of the three gifts, along with two additional typically Hungarian ingredients, marjoram and sour cream.

Serves 6

3 onions, coarsely chopped
2 cloves garlic, minced
2 bell peppers (1 red, 1 yellow), peeled and
    coarsely chopped
1½ cups chicken stock
1 tablespoon bacon fat or butter
2 tablespoons Hungarian sweet paprika
1 teaspoon dried marjoram
Salt and pepper
Pinch or 2 of cayenne pepper
1 large can (1 pound, 12 ounces) tomatoes,
    drained and chopped
5–6 medium all-purpose potatoes, such as
    round reds, peeled and cut into 1-inch
    cubes
1 pound good-quality knockwurst, sliced into
    ½-inch pieces
Sour cream
½ cup chopped fresh parsley

1. Combine the onions, garlic, peppers, ½ cup stock, and bacon fat or butter in a heavy, nonreactive pan. Cover and bring to a boil, then simmer briskly for 10 minutes. Uncover and cook for 5 minutes, or until the onions are tender and browned and the liquid has cooked away.

2. Stir in the paprika, marjoram, salt and pepper to taste, and cayenne. Stir until the vegetables are well coated with the spices, then blend in the tomatoes, potatoes, and enough stock to barely cover the contents of the pot. Bring to a boil, reduce heat, and simmer, covered, for 10 to 15 minutes, or until the potatoes are almost done.

3. Stir in the knockwurst and simmer, uncovered, for 5 to 10 additional minutes until the potatoes are completely done. Garnish with a dollop of sour cream and a sprinkling of parsley. (This dish can be made in advance, but do not add sour cream and parsley until the dish is ready to be served.)

VEGETABLE CURRY ♡

The thick, rich curry sauce in this dish is made of puréed vegetables. Although my curries are very low in fat by traditional standards, they have an authentic taste and texture. Serve this with Basmati rice, and with cold yogurt mixed with plenty of seeded, peeled, and grated cucumber, garnished with fresh coriander leaves.

Serves 6

2 large onions, cut into eighths
½ tablespoon clarified butter or margarine
Approximately 2½ cups vegetable stock
2 cloves garlic, crushed
1 red and 1 yellow bell pepper, peeled and chopped
3 carrots, peeled and coarsely chopped
¾ pound fresh mushrooms, quartered
1½ teaspoons ground cumin
1½ teaspoons ground coriander
½ teaspoon ground allspice
½ teaspoon turmeric
½ teaspoon ground ginger
¼ teaspoon cayenne pepper, or to taste
1 tablespoon tomato paste
2 medium boiling potatoes, peeled and cut into 1½-inch pieces
1 large cauliflower, trimmed and broken into large flowerets
½ large lemon
Salt
½ pound green beans, trimmed and cut into 1½-inch lengths
1 tablespoon Garam Masala (page 41)

1. Separate the segments of the onion pieces and spread them in a heavy, nonstick frying pan. Add no liquid or fat and heat the frying pan gently. Cook over moderate heat, without stirring, for 7 to 10 minutes, or until the onions are sizzling, speckled with dark amber, and beginning to stick to the pan.

2. Stir in the butter and 1 cup of the stock and let it bubble up, stirring up the browned deposits in the pan with a wooden spoon as it bubbles. Stir in the garlic, peppers, carrots, mushrooms, and spices. Turn the heat down a bit and simmer, stirring frequently, for 5 to 7 minutes, or until the mixture is very thick (not at all soupy) and the vegetables and spices are frying in the butter and their own juices. Don't rush this step; it is essential that the spices should not have a raw harsh taste. Cook very gently for a few more minutes, then stir in the tomato paste.

3. Purée half the mixture in a blender and push it through a sieve. Combine the puréed and unpuréed mixtures in the pan.

4. Add the potatoes and cauliflower. Toss everything together very well. Pour in enough remaining stock to reach about one-third of the way up the sides of the pan. Squeeze the lemon juice over the contents of the pan, season to taste with salt, and bring to a boil.

5. Reduce the heat, cover the pan, and simmer for 15 minutes. Stir in the beans and continue simmering for 5 minutes more, or until all the vegetables are tender.

6. Stir in the Garam Masala and cook for 1 minute. Serve.

Note This curry reheats very well. If you plan to cook ahead, undercook the curry slightly so the vegetables do not turn to mush when they are reheated.

POTATO STEFADO ♡

This is so easy, and it smells so enticing as it cooks. The potatoes are smothered, along with other vegetables, in a hot-and-sour mixture of wine vinegar, stock, and spices. The *stefado* is a potato adaptation of a classic Greek beef stew.

Serves 4 to 6

¾ pound mushrooms, halved or quartered depending on size
3 large all-purpose potatoes, such as round red, halved lengthwise and cut into 1½-inch chunks
8 shallots, cut into quarters or eighths depending on size
4 cloves garlic, crushed
1 large cauliflower, trimmed and broken into large flowerets
1 (6-ounce) can tomato paste
½–1 tablespoon fruity olive oil
Salt and freshly ground pepper to taste
½ cup chopped fresh parsley
1 bay leaf
1 teaspoon dried oregano
1 teaspoon ground cinnamon
1 teaspoon ground cumin
¼ cup red wine vinegar
Approximately 1 cup chicken or vegetable stock
Crumbled feta cheese, chopped fresh parsley, and chopped walnuts, for garnish

1. Preheat the oven to 350°F.

2. Combine all ingredients in a nonreactive, flameproof casserole. Bring to a boil, then remove from heat.

3. Cover tightly and bake for 1 to 1¼ hours.

4. Garnish each serving with some feta, parsley, and walnuts.

HUNGARIAN POTATO RAGOUT

I've adapted Szekely Goulash, that gorgeous Hungarian pork and sauerkraut stew, into potato-sauerkraut stew with just a touch of pork (Canadian bacon) for seasoning. This satisfies those deep corners of the soul that only good, ethnic, robust comfort food can reach.

Serves 4

1 pound sauerkraut
3 medium onions, halved and sliced into
    thin half-moons
3 cloves garlic, crushed
¼ teaspoon dried thyme
Approximately 1½ cups chicken or vegetable
    stock
¼ cup dry vermouth
1½ tablespoons butter
2 tablespoons Hungarian sweet paprika
Pinch or 2 of cayenne pepper
1 tablespoon caraway seeds
1 can (14 ounces) chopped tomatoes
2 large all-purpose potatoes, such as round
    red, halved lengthwise and cut into
    1½-inch chunks
Salt and freshly ground pepper
¼ pound Canadian bacon, sliced thin and
    chopped
Sour cream or plain yogurt

1. Preheat the oven to 350°F.

2. Drain the sauerkraut in a colander. Rinse well under cold water. Drain again and squeeze as dry as possible. Set aside.

3. Combine the onions, garlic, thyme, ¼ cup of stock, vermouth, and 1 tablespoon of butter in a heavy, nonreactive frying pan. Cover and simmer briskly for 10 minutes. Uncover and cook over moderate heat, stirring frequently, for 5 to 7 minutes, or until the liquid is almost gone and the onions are browned.

4. Off the heat, stir in the paprika, cayenne, and caraway seeds. Stir until the onions are well coated with the paprika and it has lost its raw taste.

5. Toss in the tomatoes, sauerkraut, and potatoes. Combine well, then pour the mixture into a nonreactive casserole. Season to taste with salt and pepper, and pour in enough remaining stock to just barely cover the contents. Cover closely and bake for 1 hour.

6. Meanwhile, melt the remaining butter. Gently sauté the bacon in the butter for a minute or so. After the potatoes have cooked for 1 hour, scrape the bacon mixture into the casserole and gently stir it in. Cover and bake for an additional ½ hour, or until the potatoes are very tender. (This may be refrigerated for a day or so; in fact, it mellows nicely under these circumstances.) Serve in shallow soup bowls with dollops of sour cream or yogurt.

POTATO CHILI

Chili con Patate is even better than Chili con Carne; potatoes soak up seasonings so beautifully. This is the sort of good home cooking you'll find yourself making over and over again.

Serves 4

Approximately 1½ cups chicken or vegetable stock
1 tablespoon vegetable oil
3 large onions, halved and sliced into thin half-moons
2 cloves garlic, minced
1 teaspoon crumbled dried oregano
2 tablespoons pure chili powder
1 teaspoon ground cumin
Cayenne pepper to taste
1 (6-ounce) can tomato paste
3 large all-purpose potatoes, such as round red, halved and cut into 1½-inch chunks
Salt and freshly ground pepper to taste
Grated white cheddar cheese
Sour cream or yogurt
Pepper Salad (recipe follows)

1. Combine ½ cup of the stock with the oil, onions, and garlic in a heavy skillet. Cover and simmer briskly for 10 minutes.

2. Preheat the oven to 350°F.

3. Uncover and cook for 5 to 7 minutes, or until the onions are tender and browned and the liquid has cooked away. Stir in the oregano and spices. Stir over lowest heat until the onions are well coated with the spices, then blend in the tomato paste.

4. Toss the potatoes in the onion mixture. Pour in the remaining stock, and bring to a simmer, stirring. Scrape the mixture into a casserole. Cover and bake for 1 to 1¼ hours, or until the potatoes are tender and the sauce is very thick and rich. (This reheats well but you may have to add more stock.)

5. Serve in shallow soup bowls. Top each serving with a sprinkling of cheese, a dollop of sour cream or yogurt, and a spoonful of pepper salad. Serve kidney beans on the side, if desired.

Pepper Salad

1 large green bell pepper, peeled and diced
1 large red bell pepper, peeled and diced
1 large yellow bell pepper, peeled and diced
3 thin scallions, sliced
1 tablespoon chopped fresh parsley
½ tablespoon chopped fresh coriander (optional)
Juice of ½ lime
1 tablespoon olive oil
Salt to taste
½ teaspoon sugar

Toss all the ingredients together in a bowl at least ½ hour before serving.

POTATO CURRY

East Indian cuisine is rife with wondrous potato recipes, several of which appear in this collection. Serve this one as part of an array of curries, or with a roast or a steak to give a fillip to old-fashioned "meat and potatoes."

Serves 3 to 4

1 medium onion, chopped
1 clove garlic, minced
1 tablespoon clarified butter
½ teaspoon cayenne pepper
½ teaspoon ground cumin
½ teaspoon turmeric
¼ teaspoon ground coriander
Salt
½ cup vegetable stock
1 pound new potatoes, quartered
1 teaspoon Garam Masala (page 41)
1 tablespoon lemon juice
Chopped fresh coriander

1. Sauté the onion and garlic in the butter for 5 minutes over medium heat, or until limp and transparent, but not brown.

2. Add the spices and salt to taste. Stir over lowest heat until the spices have lost their raw taste, then stir in the stock and potatoes.

3. Bring to a simmer, cover, and simmer gently for approximately 20 minutes, or until the potatoes are almost done.

4. Add the Garam Masala and lemon juice. Simmer, covered, for 10 minutes more, or until the potatoes are tender. Serve hot, garnished with coriander.

"Pray for peace and grace and spiritual food,
For wisdom and guidance, for all these are good
But don't forget the potatoes."

JOHN TYLER PETTES

VEGETABLE STUFFED PEPPERS ♡

These unusual peppers—filled with grated root vegetables, raisins, and pine nuts—make an interesting first course or a wonderful accompaniment to roasted poultry. To be perfect, the peppers must be peeled (with a swivel-bladed vegetable peeler), but don't worry if a shred of skin here and there eludes the peeler. When peeled first, the baked peppers have a voluptuous, succulent texture that is impossible to achieve with unpeeled peppers. And as they bake, the peppers leak their delicious juices into the tomato purée, creating a delicate and lovely sauce. This is very fragrant and satisfying.

Makes 12 pieces

1 teaspoon vegetable oil
Several dashes of soy sauce
1½ cups chicken or vegetable stock
¼ cup dry sherry
2 cloves garlic, crushed
1 cup coarsely grated, peeled carrot
1 cup coarsely grated, peeled white turnip
½ cup coarsely grated onion
½ cup coarsely grated all-purpose potato, such as round red (unpeeled)

½ cup pine nuts
½ cup raisins, soaked in ½ cup dry sherry for 15 minutes and drained
Salt and freshly ground pepper
¼ teaspoon grated nutmeg
6 large red or yellow peppers, peeled with a swivel-bladed peeler, halved lengthwise, and seeded
¼ cup grated Parmesan
¼ cup tomato paste

1. Preheat the oven to 350°F.

2. Heat the oil, soy sauce, ½ cup stock, and sherry in a large frying pan. Add the vegetables and toss. Cook over medium heat for 5 to 7 minutes, or until tender but not at all mushy, and the liquid is almost gone.

3. Stir in the pine nuts, raisins, salt and pepper to taste, and nutmeg. Set aside.

4. Arrange the peppers, peeled side down, in 1 or 2 baking dishes. Fill each half with an equal amount of the vegetable mixture, then sprinkle each with 1 teaspoon of Parmesan.

5. Whisk together the tomato paste and remaining stock. Pour around the peppers, cover the dish with foil, and bake for 1 hour.

Note This dish freezes very well.

BAKED SLICED POTATOES AND SPICY VEGETABLES

This is a colorful, delicious, and piquant dish, with plenty of texture and flavor contrast. It will feed fewer than you think—people can't seem to stop eating it once they start.

Serves 4

5 medium boiling potatoes, sliced thick
2 medium onions, halved and sliced into
    thick half-moons
2 large yellow bell peppers, peeled,
    stemmed, seeded, and cut into 1-inch
    chunks
3 stalks celery, cut into 2-inch pieces
2 cans (10 ounces each) tomatoes with chiles,
    drained of liquid and roughly crushed
2 tablespoons olive oil
1 teaspoon crumbled dried oregano
Salt and freshly ground pepper to taste
2 tablespoons finely chopped fresh parsley

1. Preheat the oven to 450°F.

2. Put the potatoes and onions in a bowl. Toss with the remaining ingredients. Spread the mixture in a shallow baking dish and cover tightly.

3. Bake for 30 minutes, or until the potatoes and celery are very tender.

Skillet Potatoes

"A crusty loaf of well-seasoned hashbrown pota-
toes served waist high in hot cream."
SEYMOUR BRITCHKY, Review of Gage and Tollner
The Restaurants of New York

POTATO FRITTATA

A frittata—an Italian open-faced omelet—is at its best when filled with potatoes. It pays to plan on leftover potatoes, so you can have one of these beauties for supper every so often. Try Baked Sliced Potatoes and Spicy Vegetables (page 68), Potato Curry (page 66), or any of the gratins.

Serves 4

2 tablespoons butter or olive oil
8 eggs
3 tablespoons water
Salt and freshly ground pepper
1 cup leftover sliced potatoes
Grated cheese (optional)

1. Preheat the broiler.

2. Heat the butter or oil in a 10-inch non-stick omelet pan.

3. Break the eggs into a bowl. With a fork, beat the eggs with the water and salt and pepper to taste. The yolks and whites should be very well blended, but do not overbeat or the mixture will be too thin. Stir in the potatoes.

4. Tilt the pan so that it is evenly coated with the butter or oil. Pour the egg mixture into the pan and cook over medium heat without stirring for a few moments until the eggs begin to set on the bottom.

5. With a flexible plastic spatula, lift the edge of the frittata away from the pan and tilt the pan so that the uncooked egg flows beneath the cooked portion. Continue doing this all around the pan until the frittata is almost completely set but still soft and runny in the center. If cheese is used, sprinkle it evenly over the top at this point.

6. Slide the pan under the broiler for a minute or 2 until the eggs are set and the cheese is melted. Slide out of the pan onto a warm serving plate. The frittata will look like a golden, cushiony pancake. Cut into wedges to serve. This is good served cold, too; a frittata makes splendid picnic food.

CORNED BEEF HASH, CARNEGIE DELI

The late, lamented Leo Steiner, of the famous Carnegie Deli in New York, taught me to make classic hash. If you think that corned beef hash only comes in cans and tastes like dog food, think again. The real thing is a revelation to those who experience it for the first time. At the Carnegie Deli this recipe serves 1.

Serves 4

¾ pound cooked corned beef
2 tablespoons rendered chicken fat
2 large onions, coarsely chopped
2 bell peppers, trimmed, seeded, and
    coarsely chopped
2 medium boiling potatoes, cooked, peeled,
    and coarsely chopped
Freshly ground pepper to taste

1. With a chef's knife, chop the corned beef into chunks approximately ½ inch in size. Don't worry if the chunks are not even in size. For this hash to be authentic the chunks should be rather raggedy.

2. Heat the chicken fat in a well-seasoned cast-iron skillet. Sauté the vegetables in the fat for 5 minutes or so.

3. Add the corned beef. Season generously with pepper. Toss the meat and vegetables constantly in the skillet, over moderately high heat, for 7 to 10 minutes, or until the potatoes and meat are crusty and almost burned in places. Serve plain or with poached or fried eggs.

"In the East of London in the depression potatoes formed the menus of poverty. We used to sing in Yiddish which went:
    Monday, Potatoes
    Tuesday, Potatoes
    Wednesday Potatoes, etc., etc.
    And on sabbath as a treat
    Guess what!
    A Potato Pudding."

RABBI LIONEL BLUE
Kitchen Blues

CORNED BEEF HASH MORNAY

This version of corned beef hash, served under a bubbling blanket of Mornay sauce and melted cheese, is a showstopper. Make it a star turn at Sunday brunch.

Serves 6

6 large onions, coarsely chopped
2 tablespoons (¼ stick) butter
1½ cups chicken stock
4 cups well-trimmed diced or shredded cooked corned beef
Freshly ground pepper
2 medium waxy potatoes, steamed until almost tender, peeled, and diced into 1-inch cubes
⅓ cup milk
2 cups Mornay sauce (page 56)
I cup grated Swiss

1. Combine the onions, butter, and stock in a large, heavy skillet. Cover and bring to a boil, then boil for 10 minutes. Uncover, reduce heat a bit, and boil gently, stirring occasionally, for 10 minutes, or until the onions are meltingly tender, syrupy, and amber brown. The stock should be just about gone.

2. Stir in the corned beef and grind in plenty of pepper. Add no salt; the corned beef is salty. Stir in the potatoes, then pour in the milk. Stir and cook for 5 to 7 minutes, or until the milk is absorbed, the potatoes are tender, and the mixture begins to brown slightly.

3. Spread the hash in a gratin dish. Cover with the sauce and sprinkle with cheese. (The dish can be prepared in advance and refrigerated at this point. Bring to room temperature before continuing.)

4. Preheat the oven to 400°F.

5. Bake uncovered until browned and bubbly, about ½ hour.

"I have not mashed a potato since that night of revelation. Instant mashed potatoes are as good as instant coffee is unfit to drink."

RICHARD GEHMAN
The Haphazard Gourmet, 1966

LATKES

These may be the best potato pancakes in the world, if not the universe. The secret is to use a hand-grater, and grate the raw potato into *long* strips.

Serves 6

6 medium baking potatoes
2 eggs
1 onion
1½ teaspoons salt
½ cup unbleached all-purpose flour
Oil or clarified butter
Sour cream or applesauce

1. Scrub the potatoes. (It is not necessary to peel them.) Grate them in long strips, using the large holes on a 4-sided grater, into a bowl of cold water.

2. Beat the eggs in a bowl. Grate the onion into the beaten eggs, then stir in the salt and flour.

3. Drain the potatoes very well, squeezing out all excess moisture. Add the potatoes to the egg-flour mixture, and stir well.

4. Pour the oil into a wide, heavy skillet to about ½ inch deep. Heat until hot but not smoking. Drop the potato mixture into the hot oil by the heaping tablespoon. Flatten each dollop of batter into a flat pancake, and fry on each side until golden brown and crisp. Drain on paper towels. Serve at once with sour cream or applesauce.

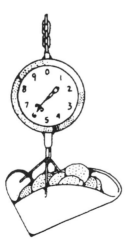

ROESTI

Roesti is a large, grated-potato pancake, cooked gently until the bottom of the pancake is crusty and browned. You need a trusty, well-seasoned skillet for this, so that the bottom of the pancake does not stick and burn. Turned out onto a plate, with its golden, crusty side up, Roesti is a dazzling sight.

Serves 6

4 large baking potatoes
½ cup (1 stick) butter
Salt and pepper to taste
3 tablespoons hot water or stock

1. Boil the potatoes in water to cover for about 30 minutes, or until tender but not falling apart. Drain and cool in the refrigerator, preferably overnight.

2. Peel the potatoes and shred them into long strips, as long as possible, using the large holes on a grater.

3. Melt the butter in a large, well-seasoned cast-iron or enameled skillet with a lid. Add the potatoes and seasoning, and stir gently with a spatula until butter is absorbed.

4. Lightly press potatoes down in the pan with the spatula. Sprinkle the hot water over the potatoes and cover the skillet. Cook over a moderately low heat for 30 to 45 minutes. The potatoes should form a beautifully crusty brown bottom. Check heat frequently so potatoes do not burn.

5. When done, loosen the potato cake all around with a spatula and turn out onto a plate, crusty side up. Serve at once.

"**Roesti is a Swiss grated-potato dish. In reality it is an excuse for eating a quarter of a pound of butter.**"

LAURIE COLWIN
Gourmet magazine, 1986

Roasted and Fried

"Americans, contrary to what we may have
been told, are once again becoming a
meat-and-potatoes crowd."
Gourmet magazine, December 1987

ROASTED NEW POTATOES WITH ONIONS AND GARLIC♡

The perceptive reader will, by now, have noticed my extreme fondness for garlic. It's no secret; I love it, particularly in quantity. While some people add a clove or two to a sauce, wondering nervously all the while if they are erring on the side of excess, I throw in the cloves by the double handful. Keep this in mind: the glorious bulb is a vegetable, meant to be used in exhilarating quantity. And garlic, gently cooked by braising or roasting, becomes soft, buttery, and mild. If you're still not convinced, try roasting potatoes on a bed of garlic and onions. As this cooks, the aroma is almost unbearable, it's so good.

Serves 4

1 head garlic
3 medium onions, halved and sliced into thin half-moons
8 medium new potatoes, unpeeled, cut in half
Approximately ⅓ cup chicken or vegetable stock
Salt and freshly ground pepper
1 tablespoon butter or margarine

1. Preheat the oven to 400°F.

2. Separate the head of garlic into cloves. Hit each clove lightly with a kitchen mallet to loosen the skin. Remove and discard the skin. Scatter the garlic cloves and the onion slices on the bottom of a baking dish that will hold the halved potatoes in 1 layer.

3. Place the halved potatoes, cut sides down, on the bed of garlic and onions. Pour in enough stock to come about one-quarter of the way up the sides of the dish. Sprinkle salt and pepper evenly over all, then dot with butter.

4. Bake, uncovered, for 1 hour, or until the potatoes are tender, the onions beginning to brown, and the liquid about gone. Serve piping hot.

INDIAN ROAST POTATOES

It's always such a pleasure to add spices to potatoes; the spuds take to interesting spicing as the proverbial duck takes to water. Do be sure, however, that you gently cook the spices first in a little bit of oil or butter so that they lose their raw harshness.

Serves 2 to 4

2 tablespoons clarified butter
1 medium onion, cut into eighths
1 teaspoon ground cumin
1 teaspoon ground coriander
¼ teaspoon cayenne pepper
4 medium boiling potatoes, quartered
Approximately ¼ cup chicken or vegetable
    stock
Salt and freshly ground pepper to taste
Chopped fresh coriander
Wedges of fresh lime

1. Preheat the oven to 400°F.

2. Heat the butter in a skillet over medium heat. Toss the onion quickly in the hot butter until they begin to wilt. Add the spices and toss over lowest heat until the onion is well coated with the spices and spices have lost their raw taste. Add the potatoes and toss so that everything is well combined. Scrape the mixture into a shallow baking dish that can hold the potatoes in 1 layer.

3. Stir in the stock and bake for 1 hour, uncovered, stirring every 15 minutes or so. Add a bit more stock if necessary from time to time, but the finished dish should be very dry. Serve with chopped coriander and wedges of lime.

"**Did you know that they [the Incas] measured their units of time by the time it takes a potato to cook?**"

JANE GRIGSON
The Vegetable Book

ROSEMARY POTATOES

Here's a variation on the roasted potato and garlic theme, with rosemary beautifully complementing the garlic.

Serves 4

1 head garlic, separated into cloves
4 tablespoons (½ stick) butter, melted and clarified
4 medium boiling potatoes, quartered
Salt and pepper
1½ teaspoons dried rosemary
¼ cup chicken or vegetable stock

1. Preheat the oven to 400°F.

2. Crush each garlic clove lightly with a kitchen mallet. Remove the skin.

3. Pour the butter into a baking dish that will hold the potatoes in 1 layer. Scatter in the garlic, then add the potatoes, salt and pepper to taste, rosemary, and stock. Toss with 2 spoons to coat the potatoes and garlic with the butter and rosemary. Bake, uncovered, for approximately 1 hour, stirring everything up every 15 minutes or so.

VARIATION Substitute olive oil and a generous squeeze of lemon juice for the butter, and oregano or a mixture of oregano and basil for the rosemary.

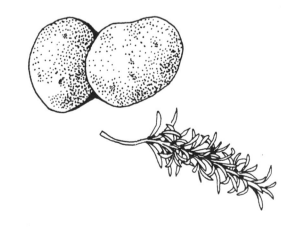

"Straight from the vast convention floor of Snaxpo 186, the international conclave of the snack food industry, comes a spicy sociological morsel to chew on; the potato chip has withstood the United States nutrition crunch."
Washington Post, 1987

OVEN "FRIES" ♡

I hate deep-frying. It's messy, smelly, unhealthy, and fattening. But crisp, brown fried potatoes are necessities of life. How nice to be able to "fry" them in the oven with the bare minimum of fat. They are even better than conventionally fried spuds because you taste *potatoes* not a mouthful of grease.

Serves 4 to 6

2 pounds Idaho baking potatoes
¾–1 tablespoon vegetable oil
Salt

1. Preheat the oven to 500°F. Place 1 large or 2 smaller nonstick baking sheets in the oven.

2. Working quickly, slice the unpeeled potatoes lengthwise into ½-inch-thick slices. Quickly cut each slice lengthwise into ¼-inch-wide strips. Toss these strips in a bowl with the oil. Quickly spread them, in a single layer, on the hot baking sheets.

3. Bake for 20 to 30 minutes. Then turn each strip with tongs and bake for another 10 to 15 minutes, until crisp, golden brown, and cooked through. Sprinkle with salt and serve at once.

CHIPS AHOY

In Saratoga, New York, earlier in the century, a jaded restaurant diner sent back his fried potatoes, complaining that they were too thick. The chef cut thinner slices, fried them, and sent them out. "Too thick," insisted the diner, and he rejected them out of hand. The chef went into a snit. He seized a potato, cut it paper thin, fried the gossamer slices until they were impossibly brittle, and dispatched them with a sneer. The diner was not insulted. In fact, he was enchanted, as was everyone else by the crunchy, incredibly thin, shatter-in-the-mouth morsels. Instant sensation! The potato chip was born. Over the years, the now familiar chip has lost a good bit of its purity. Stroll through supermarkets and specialty stores, and you will find a bewildering array of potato chips, from sausage-and-tomato flavor to chocolate covered. But search further and you will see that small independent chippers here and there (like the Cape Cod Company in Massachusetts) are beginning to make lovely, old-fashioned chips again. Sweet potato chips are coming into favor, too—delicious, crunchy orange morsels.

HERBED OVEN "FRIED" POTATO SLICES ♡

Slicing the potatoes and seasoning them with herbs before baking completely changes the character of oven "fries."

Serves 4 to 6

2 pounds large Idaho Russet potatoes
1 tablespoon olive oil
1 teaspoon crumbled mixed dried oregano
    and basil
Salt

1. Preheat the oven to 500°F. Place a large nonstick baking sheet in the oven.

2. Cut the unpeeled potatoes crosswise into ¼-inch-thick slices. Toss the slices with the oil and herbs.

3. Spread slices on the hot sheet. Bake for 20 to 30 minutes.

4. Turn and bake 10 to 15 minutes more, until crusty, golden, and done. Sprinkle with salt and serve at once.

VARIATION This recipe works well with sweet potatoes instead of Idaho Russets.

"What holiday is sacred to all potatoes?
Mash Wednesday."

PAUL McMAHON
Potato Jokes

Salads

"Rebecca Dew's a good cook and a genius with cold potatoes."

LUCY MAUDE MONTGOMERY
Anne of Windy Poplars

SPICY POTATO SALAD ♡

Potato salad is so good made with an interesting spice mix and a yogurt-buttermilk mixture instead of mayonnaise. There are countless ways of doing it, and they all make a welcome change from the cliché of potato salad—hard-boiled eggs, mayonnaise, and celery.

Serves 6

1½ pounds boiling potatoes, unpeeled,
    steamed until tender but not mushy
2 tablespoons fresh lime juice
1 teaspoon soy sauce
¼ teaspoon cayenne pepper
½ teaspoon ground cumin
1 teaspoon caraway seeds
2 stalks celery, diced
1 carrot, coarsely grated
½ small red pepper, peeled and diced
½ small yellow pepper, peeled and diced
Salt and freshly ground pepper to taste
Dressing

1. Cool the potatoes to lukewarm. Cut into 1-inch cubes, then toss with the lime juice, soy sauce, and spices.

2. Gently combine potato mixture with the remaining ingredients. Pour dressing over and fold in. Chill until ready to serve.

Dressing
3 tablespoons yogurt
1 tablespoon buttermilk
3 scallions, trimmed and sliced thin
1 tablespoon snipped fresh chives
1 tablespoon chopped fresh parsley

Combine thoroughly.

CHICK-PEA AND POTATO SALAD♡

Another yogurt-spice potato salad, with chick-peas added to complement the potatoes.

Serves 6

1 pound new potatoes, unpeeled
1 can chick-peas
2 tablespoons fresh lime juice
1 teaspoon soy sauce
1 tablespoon vegetable oil
½ teaspoon ground cumin
½ teaspoon crushed, dried chiles
4 scallions, trimmed and sliced thinly
3 tablespoons chopped fresh parsley
2 tablespoons yogurt
1 tablespoon buttermilk

1. Steam the potatoes for 7 to 10 minutes, until tender but not mushy. Cut into ½-inch cubes while still warm.

2. Drain and rinse the chick-peas. Combine in a bowl with the potatoes.

3. Stir together the lime juice, soy sauce, oil, and spices, then add mixture to the potatoes. Toss gently with 2 spoons so that potatoes absorb the liquid. Stir in the scallions and parsley.

4. Blend together the yogurt and buttermilk. Gently fold the mixture into the potatoes. Serve warm or chilled.

"No one has feared developing leprosy from eating French Fries, or any form of potato, ever since that brave Frenchman Parmentier disproved that possibility a few centuries back."

JAMES VILLAS
American Taste

CURRIED POTATO CAULIFLOWER SALAD

Potato and cauliflower make an excellent combination, one often found in East Indian cooking. Here the two vegetables are folded into a spicy dressing. It's good warm or at room temperature.

Serves 8 to 10

7 shallots, peeled and chopped
1 cup golden raisins
½ cup chicken or vegetable stock
½ cup raspberry vinegar
2 tablespoons vegetable oil
2 teaspoons minced fresh ginger
1 clove garlic, minced
1 teaspoon turmeric
2 teaspoons each ground cumin, coriander, and cinnamon
Pinch of ground cloves
½ teaspoon ground allspice
¼ teaspoon cayenne (ground red) pepper
3 tablespoons plain yogurt
3 tablespoons sour cream
2 tablespoons buttermilk
Salt and freshly ground pepper
1 head cauliflower, trimmed, broken into flowerets, and steamed
1 pound boiling potatoes, steamed and cut into 1½-inch cubes
½ cup chopped fresh parsley

1. Spread the shallot pieces in a heavy frying pan. Add *no* liquid or fat, and heat gently. Cook over moderate heat, without stirring, for 3 to 4 minutes, or until the shallots are sizzling, speckled with dark amber, and beginning to stick to the pan.

2. Stir in the raisins, stock, and vinegar, and let liquid bubble up, stirring up any browned deposits with a wooden spoon.

3. Stir in the oil, ginger, garlic, and spices. Cook very gently for 5 minutes, or until the shallots are well coated with the spices, the spices have lost their raw taste, and the stock is about gone. Cool slightly.

4. Blend together the shallot mixture, yogurt, sour cream, buttermilk, and salt and pepper to taste. Toss the mixture with the warm potatoes and cauliflower, then stir in the parsley just before serving.

WARM SAUSAGE AND POTATO SALAD

This is an excellent main-dish winter potato salad. Steaming the knockwurst and the potatoes together gives the spuds a ravishing flavor.

Serves 4

1 pound knockwurst, sliced ¼ inch thick
1 pound new potatoes, quartered
Mustard Vinaigrette
¼ teaspoon crumbled dried thyme
1 tablespoon drained capers
½ tablespoon sliced scallions
½ cup chopped fresh parsley

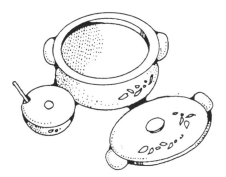

1. Steam the knockwurst and potatoes together for 10 minutes, or until the potatoes are tender.

2. Immediately blend them gently with the vinaigrette. Toss in remaining ingredients. Serve warm or at room temperature.

Mustard Vinaigrette
3 tablespoons red wine vinegar
1 clove garlic, crushed
1 tablespoon Dijon mustard
6 tablespoons olive oil
Salt and freshly ground pepper

1. Combine the vinegar and garlic in a bowl. With a small wire whisk, beat in the mustard.

2. Drizzle in the oil in a very thin stream, beating all the while. The mixture should be thick, creamy, and emulsified. Season to taste with a frugal amount of salt and freshly ground pepper.

CHICKEN AND PESTO POTATO SALAD ♡

This chicken salad—smoked chicken and potatoes in a red pepper-studded creamy basil sauce—will be the star of any buffet or summer meal. You *must* have fresh basil. Grow it yourself; if you provide a sunny window and good music, the herb will thrive.

Serves 6

1 pound small new potatoes
1 pound skinned, boned, and cubed smoked chicken
1 red bell pepper, peeled and coarsely chopped
½ cup Creamy Pesto
¼ cup buttermilk
Whole basil leaves, for garnish

1. Cut the potatoes into halves or quarters, depending on size. Do not peel. Steam over boiling water for 5 to 7 minutes, until cooked through but not mushy. Cool.

2. Cut potatoes into 1-inch chunks. Combine chicken and pepper.

3. Thin the pesto to a dressing consistency with a bit of buttermilk. Toss the potato-chicken mixture with the pesto. Serve on a platter, garnished with basil leaves.

Creamy Pesto

Because the garlic is roasted first, the garlic taste is very gentle and mellow. This is an extraordinary version of pesto. Try it spread on black bread and topped with smoked salmon.

Makes 1½ cups

2 cups torn fresh basil leaves
1¼ cups roughly chopped fresh parsley
5 tablespoons freshly grated Parmesan
1 ounce pine nuts
½ pound low-fat ricotta
Purée from 2 heads of roasted garlic (page 35)
Salt and freshly ground pepper to taste

1. Combine all ingredients in the container of a food processor.

2. Process to a thick paste. Scrape into a bowl and refrigerate.

GREEN BEANS AND POTATOES WITH SUN-DRIED TOMATOES

How did we survive before sun-dried tomatoes? Now that I've been using them regularly, I don't think I could live happily without them. This salad embodies the soul of the Mediterranean.

Serves 6

2 pounds green beans, trimmed
¾ cup chicken stock
¼ cup olive oil (use some of the oil from the sun-dried tomatoes, if packed in oil)
2 large cloves garlic, minced
1 large onion, chopped
4 small ripe tomatoes, peeled, seeded, juiced, and coarsely chopped
6 sun-dried tomatoes, chopped coarsely
1 tablespoon shredded fresh basil
Salt and freshly ground pepper to taste
¼ cup wine vinegar
½ cup chopped fresh parsley
4 small new potatoes, steamed and quartered
1 tablespoon drained capers

1. Place the beans in a heavy pot. Add the stock, oil, garlic, and onion. Stir well to combine.

2. Bring to a boil. Reduce heat slightly, and cook, covered, over moderate heat for 5 minutes, uncovering to stir frequently.

3. Add the fresh and sun-dried tomatoes. Stir and cook over moderately high heat for 5 to 7 minutes, or until the beans are cooked but not mushy. Uncover to stir frequently during this cooking time; do not overcook the beans.

4. Transfer the beans and pan juices to a bowl. Add the remaining ingredients and toss gently to thoroughly combine. Allow the beans to stand at room temperature for an hour or so for the flavors to develop.

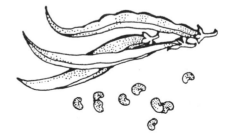

ALOO RAITA ♡

The small amount of clarified butter here gives a very special texture to this East Indian potato dish. A *raita* is a kind of sauce-salad, meant to be served with curries, especially very hot ones.

Makes 3¾ cups

4 medium boiling potatoes
1 medium onion, chopped
1 teaspoon clarified butter or margarine
½ teaspoon ground coriander
1 teaspoon ground cumin
¼ teaspoon cayenne pepper
2 cups yogurt, at room temperature
Salt and freshly ground pepper
2 tablespoons coarsely chopped fresh mint,
    for garnish

1. Steam the potatoes for 10 minutes, or until tender but not mushy. Cut into ¾-inch cubes and put in a bowl.

2. Sauté the onion in clarified butter until tender. Add the coriander, cumin, and cayenne. Stir over lowest heat for a few moments, until the onions are coated with the spices and the spices have lost their raw taste. Scrape this mixture over the potatoes.

3. Pour the yogurt over the potatoes. Mix gently. Season to taste and garnish with mint.

SADIE'S PEPITAS

One of my happiest potato experiences happened in a bowling alley. Sadie's, a hotbed of lusty New Mexican cuisine, is tucked away in an Albuquerque bowling alley. There amidst the sound of thundering balls and flying pins, I once feasted on Sadie's Pepitas, a huge plateful of fried potatoes awash in fiery red chili sauce. To make your own version of Sadie's Pepitas, prepare the Chunky Tomato Sauce, adding chopped fresh chiles and a touch of cumin and pure chili powder in Step 1. How many chiles? It depends on your taste, but this dish was designed for those with asbestos palates, so be cautious. Swamp a large plateful of Oven "Fries" (page 79) with the sauce and sprinkle with chopped coriander leaves. You'll be bowled over!

Desserts

"I wouldn't be surprised to hear that someone has come out with an all-potato diet that would permit all of the potatoes the dieter could stuff down—french fried, cottage fried, home fried, mashed, shoe-string, latkes, dumplings—as long as he puts nothing else to his lips except 14 quarts of water a day."

CALVIN TRILLIN
American Fried

CHOCOLATE-POTATO TORTE

This mousselike torte is a classic in my family. I serve it often to guests. They savor it with deep sighs and eye-rolling appreciation until I feel impelled to announce, proudly, the secret ingredient. Then they stop eating and look pained. So serve it to your best gourmet friends, but don't tell them every little detail. What they don't know won't hurt them.

Serves approximately 12

5 ounces unsweetened chocolate
1 teaspoon instant coffee powder
½ cup (1 stick) butter, softened
1½ cups sugar
5 egg yolks
1 teaspoon orange extract
2 cups hot mashed potatoes (instant mashed potatoes work fine)
Whipped cream (optional)

1. Line a 4-cup shallow baking dish with parchment paper.

2. Melt the chocolate with the coffee in the top of a double boiler set over simmering water.

3. Cream the butter with an electric mixer. Beat in the sugar, then beat in the yolks, 1 at a time. Beat very well.

4. Beat in the chocolate-coffee mixture and the orange extract, then the potatoes.

5. Spread the mixture in the prepared dish. Smooth the top and cover with waxed paper. Refrigerate for 24 hours, then serve cut in thin slices, with whipped cream, if desired.

WOULD YOU BELIEVE?

Are you convinced that potatoes and chocolate are a marriage made in heaven? Have your food inhibitions and prejudices given way enough to embrace the odd but delightful notion that potato fanatic-chocoholics can enjoy their two favorite foodstuffs in one glorious blow out? Good. But wait—relax those hardened preconceptions even more. How do you feel about ice cream? If your passion for ice cream matches your passion for potatoes, you will be delighted to know that Reed's Dairy (in Idaho, of course) has come up with Al and Reed's All Natural Ice Cream. The cold confection is billed as being sugar-free, completely natural, and relatively low in calories. And (be still my palpitating heart) it's made with potatoes. Now, if someone would just add a little garlic. . . .

CHOCOLATE-POTATO PÂTÉ

This is an elegant block of textured, dark, creamy chocolate. The texture comes from ground almonds and crushed Petite Beurre biscuits, the rich creaminess from the chocolate *and* the potatoes.

Serves 12

1½ pounds semisweet chocolate
2 eggs
⅓ cup superfine sugar
1 cup (2 sticks) butter, melted
1 tablespoon strong coffee
1 cup cooked, peeled, and riced baking potatoes
2 cups crushed Petite Beurre biscuits
1 cup ground almonds
Whipped cream or raspberry sauce

1. Line a loaf pan with waxed paper or baking parchment. Coat it with vegetable spray or oil it very lightly.

2. Melt the chocolate. Set aside.

3. Beat the eggs with the sugar until they are thick and creamy and lemon colored. Gently stir in the butter, then the chocolate, coffee, potatoes, biscuits, and ground almonds. Mix well.

4. Chill in refrigerator to firm for 1½ to 2 hours.

5. Pour the mixture into the loaf tin. Smooth the top. Rap it smartly on the countertop to eliminate air bubbles. Cover and refrigerate for at least 2 days. To serve, turn loaf out of the pan and peel away the paper. Cut into very thin slices. Serve with a dollop of whipped cream or a pool of raspberry sauce made by sieving fresh or frozen raspberries and sweetening to taste.

"Forget caviar and candy for once, why not give potatoes for Christmas?"

LYNDA BROWN
The Guardian, 1987

CHOCOLATE ICING

This is an old-fashioned cocoa icing: rich-tasting and evocative of childhood chocolate cakes.

Makes enough to frost the top and between the layers of an 8-inch cake

½ cup (1 stick) butter, softened
¼ cup cooked, peeled, and riced baking potato
¼ cup unsweetened cocoa powder
2 cups confectioners' sugar

1. Place the butter and potato in a mixing bowl.

2. Sift together the cocoa and sugar. Beat the mixture into the potatoes until light and fluffy.

LEMON CREAM FILLING

Yes, potatoes *are* versatile. I received this recipe from the British Potato Board, and it's true: one would never know that this light, fluffy, and lemony icing contains potatoes.

Makes enough for one 8-inch cake

1¾ cups confectioners' sugar
4 tablespoons (½ stick) butter, softened
¼ cup cooked, peeled, and riced baking potatoes
½ tablespoon lemon juice

1. Beat the confectioners' sugar and butter into a smooth cream.

2. Beat in the riced potatoes and the lemon juice. Spread between the layers of a sponge cake.

CHOCOLATE-POTATO TRUFFLES

Chocolate and potatoes—two pre-Columbian treasures from Latin America—were made to be eaten together. You don't believe me? I insist that you try it. Face it, you haven't lived (gastronomically speaking) until you have tried chocolate-spud truffles (these chocolate truffles really *are* earthy) or a French-style Chocolate-Potato Torte (page 90). Just don't babble about their potato content; people tend to get nervous.

Makes approximately 30 truffles

2 ounces unsweetened chocolate
5 ounces semisweet chocolate
1½ tablespoons butter
2 tablespoons Grand Marnier or Cointreau
1 egg yolk
½ cup ground almonds
¼ cup cooked, peeled, and riced baking potatoes
1 cup confectioners' sugar
Unsweetened Dutch-process cocoa

1. Melt together the chocolate and butter. Remove from the heat and cool slightly.

2. Stir in the orange brandy or liqueur and the egg yolk.

3. Thoroughly stir in the remaining ingredients except the cocoa.

4. Chill the mixture for about 1 hour.

5. Roll chocolate mixture into balls of about ¾-inch diameter. Toss each ball in the cocoa powder. Store truffles in the refrigerator, but leave at room temperature for 10 minutes before serving.

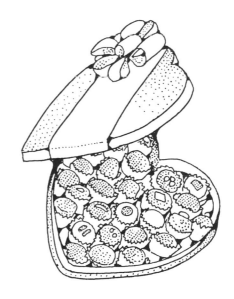

Index